Our American Century

★

The American Dream · The 50s

★

By the Editors of Time-Life Books, Alexandria, Virginia

With a Foreword by Hugh Downs

Contents

★

A group of children tries with varying success to imitate a University of Michigan drum major rehearsing his high kicks in Ann Arbor in 1950.

Foreword

Looking at the marvelous old images in this book unleashed a flood of memories of the 1950s. For many in my generation those were exciting days when the sky seemed the limit. We had experienced the Great Depression in the 1930s and world war in the 1940s, and we were weary of poverty and strife. I grew up on a little truck farm in Ohio where we never went hungry but didn't have any frills. I felt I had no way to go but up. I started out in radio when I was only 18, and at first I thought television was a gimmick like 3-D movies that would just go away. In 1945 I did an experimental TV newscast in Chicago, when there were fewer than 400 sets in the whole metropolitan area. Most of them were in bars, so I figured I was just talking to a bunch of drunks. But then television began mesmerizing lots of people, and I got into it. I was work-

ing in Chicago for NBC when my first regular TV show got knocked off the network by a pianist out of Milwaukee with only one name: Liberace. I moved to New York, where I later teamed up with a guy named Jack Paar on *The Tonight Show.*

I was fulfilling my own version of the American dream. It's easy now to forget the dark side—the conformity and the paranoid concern about Communism. So many people in the entertainment industry were being blacklisted for supposed Communist connections that a colleague in Chicago warned me it wasn't even safe to subscribe to *Consumer Reports* magazine. Some nuts, he told me, thought that anybody who would bypass the traditional way of evaluating products through advertising must be a pinko. That scared me. Later, when I was making my way through the Great Books reading program and got to Karl Marx's *Das Kapital,* I didn't have the nerve to read it on the New York subway without a plain brown wrapper. Mostly, however, I remember a feeling of hope and optimism. We just took it for granted that everything was going to be okay—and marched off into the future. In *The American Dream* you'll find the spirit of those days.

Hugh Downs

To show how fast the suburbs were growing, *Life* magazine created this 1952 image of moving vans jamming a street in Lakewood, California. New, postwar neighborhoods like Lakewood transformed the American landscape during the 1950s.

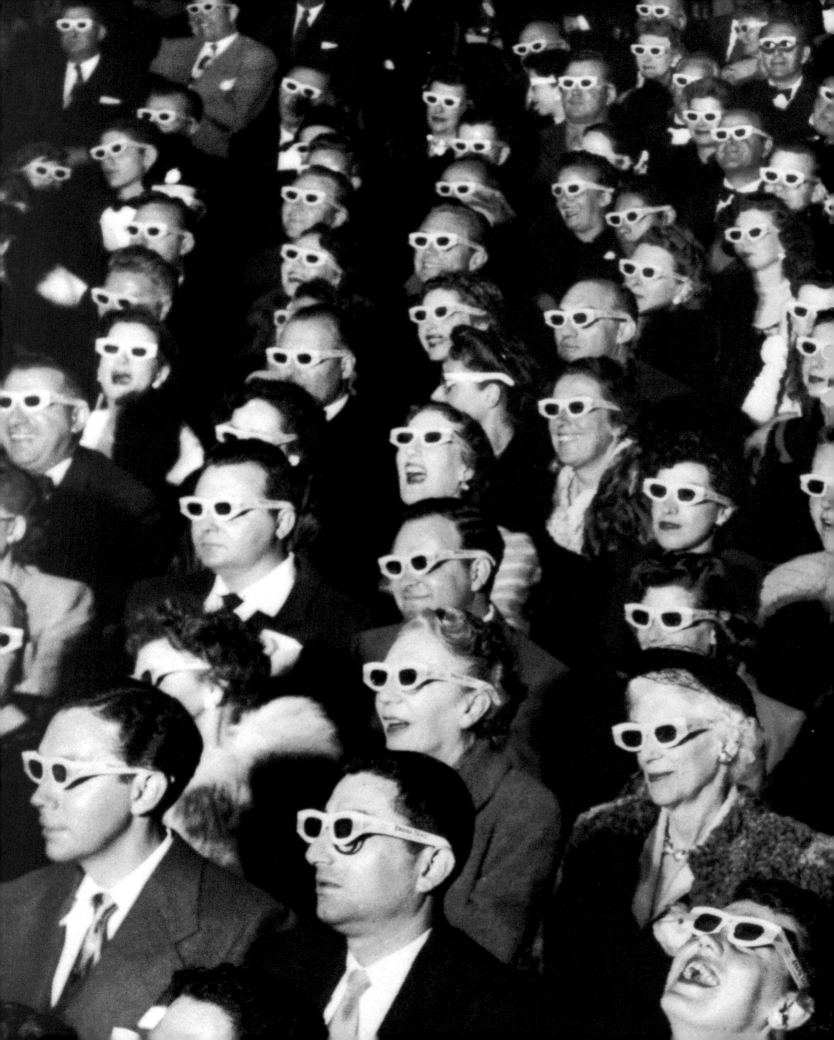

A packed audience wears special glasses to enjoy
1952's *Bwana Devil*, the first 3-D movie. Invented
to create the illusion of depth, the process could make
objects appear to dart out at startled moviegoers.

In December 1950, a line of U.S. marines winds through North Korean hills on a 40-mile march to the sea. Temperatures that winter reached 20 below zero.

Only inches from a crowd of eager fans, rock and roll sensation Elvis Presley electrifies a Miami, Florida, audience with his hit song "Hound Dog" in August 1956. A local pigeon, visible just above his hand, roosts quietly through all the fuss.

Little Leaguers, including one boy too antsy to sit still, await the missing parts of their uniforms in a Manchester, New Hampshire, classroom in 1954. Children's sports and scouting were both tremendously popular in the 1950s.

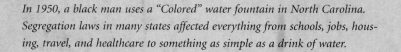

COLORED

In 1950, a black man uses a "Colored" water fountain in North Carolina. Segregation laws in many states affected everything from schools, jobs, housing, travel, and healthcare to something as simple as a drink of water.

In the summer of 1955, a cherished Dalmatian stands proudly in a Ford Fairlane painted to match his spotted coat. Cars of the 1950s often expressed their owners' tastes, but usually not so literally.

The Best of Times: 1950-1959

Future historians would have no problem pinpointing the whereabouts of nearly one-third of the American nation at 9 p.m. (EST) on Monday, January 19, 1953. Some 44 million men, women, and children out of a U.S. population of 158 million were gathered in front of television sets from coast to coast. Onto hundreds of thousands of tiny screens flashed the flickering black-and-white images that everyone who loved Lucy had been waiting for: Lucy was having a baby. Lucy, of course, was Lucille Ball, the star of *I Love Lucy*. It was the most popular show on television, the new medium that was changing the United States like no invention since the automobile. Lucy was a ditsy housewife. Her husband on the show, Ricky Ricardo, was her real-life spouse, Desi Arnaz, a Cuban bandleader on and off the screen. Many American viewers, newly moved away from family and friends to the suburbs, felt they knew Lucy and Ricky better than they knew their neighbors.

To this generation of young suburbanites, it was no great surprise when Lucille Ball became pregnant in the spring of 1952. The United States was nearing the peak of that most prolific period in the nation's history known as the baby boom. The real-life Lucy and her husband saw immediately that her pregnancy would make a wonderful plot device, but they had a hard time convincing CBS executives, who feared that some fans would consider the subject in poor taste. The nervous network bent over backward to avoid offending them, hiring a minister, a priest, and a rabbi to review every script.

Lucy and Desi, it turned out, knew their viewers. They also knew the kind of male-female repartee that passed for humor in those days, when husbands were supposed to be all-knowing and wives naive or scatter-brained or both. "I want to tell you something," Lucy announced in the episode of December 8, 1952. "Uh-oh," Ricky replied, "how much are you overdrawn?" Her on-air pregnancy progressed through morning sickness, late-night cravings for sardine-and-hot-fudge-covered pistachio ice cream, and Ricky's own imaginary labor pains. Then, on January 19, 1953—the same day that Lucille Ball delivered son Desi Jr. (actually, Desiderio Alberto Arnaz y de Acha IV)—two-thirds of the television sets in America tuned

A Timeline of the 50s

1950

The Brink's armored car depot *in Boston is robbed of $2.7 million, the largest amount stolen in a robbery to date.*

Alger Hiss, *a State Department official under investigation for his Communist ties, is convicted of perjury and sentenced to a five-year prison term.*

President Harry Truman *orders the Atomic Energy Committee to develop the hydrogen bomb.*

Ted Williams *of the Boston Red Sox becomes baseball's highest-paid player, with a $125,000 contract.*

Senator Joseph R. McCarthy, *in a speech before a women's group in Wheeling, West Virginia, claims to have a list containing the names of 205 known Communists in the State Department.*

The FBI *issues its first list of the Ten Most Wanted Criminals.*

The U.S. Postmaster General *cuts mail delivery from twice to once a day.*

Televised hearings *on organized crime begin in May before the Senate Crime Investigating Committee, chaired by Senator Estes Kefauver.*

The first transplant of a kidney *from one human to another is performed on a 49-year-old woman at a Chicago hospital.*

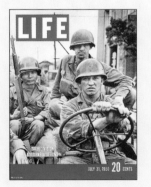

The North Korean People's Army *invades South Korea. United Nations forces under General Douglas MacArthur join South Korea in the war.*

United Nations mediator *Dr. Ralph J. Bunche wins the Nobel Peace Prize for negotiating an end to the Arab-Israeli war.*

Two Puerto Rican nationalists *attempt to assassinate President Truman in Washington, D.C.*

Charles M. Schulz's comic strip *"Peanuts" makes its debut in eight newspapers.*

Smokey the Bear, *an orphaned cub found after a forest fire in New Mexico, becomes the living symbol of the U.S. Forestry Service.*

New on TV: *"The Jack Benny Show"; "What's My Line?"; "You Bet Your Life"; "Your Show of Shows."*

New in Print: *"Betty Crocker's Picture Cook Book."*

New Products: *Miss Clairol hair coloring; Minute Rice; prefabricated fallout shelters; Diners Club credit card; Xerox copy machine.*

The Academy Awards: *best picture—"All About Eve"; best actor—José Ferrer for "Cyrano de Bergerac"; best actress—Judy Holliday for "Born Yesterday."*

1951

The 22nd Amendment *to the Constitution, limiting the presidency to two terms, is adopted.*

Margaret Sanger, *pioneer of birth control, urges development of an oral contraceptive.*

Stripped of his commands *in Asia by President Truman, General Douglas MacArthur, speaking before Congress, closes out his 52 years of military service by proclaiming, "Old soldiers never die; they just fade away."*

The average cost *of four years of college is $1,800, an increase of 400 percent since 1900.*

Sugar Ray Robinson *defeats Jake "Raging Bull" LaMotta for the middleweight championship of the world.*

in to witness the previously filmed arrival of the fictional Little Ricky.

It was the highest rating in the history of the young medium. By contrast, only about half as many sets were turned on the following day when the enormously popular war hero Dwight David Eisenhower was inaugurated as the 34th president of the United States. Like Lucy during her pregnancy, the nation was expectant, swelling with the feeling that things were good and would get even better.

An Inauspicious Beginning: The dawn of the decade had not appeared so hopeful. The escalating Cold War with the Soviet Union cast such deep shadows that some Americans considered 1950 the darkest time since early World War II.

A series of cataclysms rocked the nation that year. President Harry Truman ordered development of a superbomb that would dwarf in destructive power the atomic bombs dropped on Hiroshima and Nagasaki during the war against Japan. Alger Hiss, a former State Department official accused of stealing government documents during the 1930s, was convicted of perjury. A spy ring that actually had given atomic bomb secrets to the Soviets during the war started to unravel, leading to the execution of Julius and Ethel Rosenberg for espionage. U.S. Senator Joseph McCarthy of Wisconsin embarked upon a crusade to ferret out subversives that would ruin innocent lives and end only after television exposed his brutal tactics *(pages 80-81)*.

The worst blow of 1950 came in June, when the Soviet-aided army of North Korea invaded South Korea. Truman sent U.S. troops and gained backing from the United Nations. But after the Chinese Communists intervened, it became a three-year war that no one would win—much to the frustration of Americans accustomed to victory *(pages 82-85)*.

Happier Days: The inauguration of President Eisenhower in 1953 heralded the coming of better times. Ike concluded an armistice in the stalemated Korean War that summer. Cold War anxieties eased a little under the glow of a new optimism and unprecedented prosperity. This was the true beginning of what so many would recall fondly as the nifty '50s, the period later immortalized in the movie *American Graffiti*—set in the early 1960s, but rich with music and memories from the 1950s—and then the television show *Happy Days*.

With his wide grin and the disarming nickname by which he was known universally, Ike was a unifier. His genial, father-knows-best manner

UNIVAC, *the first general-purpose electronic computer, is dedicated at the Census Bureau in Philadelphia.*

AT&T *becomes the world's first corporation to have over one million stockholders.*

CBS introduces color television *in a program hosted by Ed Sullivan (above) and Arthur Godfrey.*

New York Yankee Joe DiMaggio *hangs up his glove and retires with a lifetime batting average of .325 and a total of 361 home runs.*

Flouridation *in the water, according to the U.S. Public Health Service, greatly reduces tooth decay.*

Lacoste tennis shirts with the alligator symbol are introduced in the U.S. by French manufacturer Izod.

Earl Tupper *creates the home sales party to market his plastic food storage containers directly to householders.*

New in Print: *"Jet" newsmagazine; Herman Wouk's "The Caine Mutiny"; J. D. Salinger's "The Catcher in the Rye."*

New on TV: *"Search for Tomorrow"; "Love of Life"; "The Red Skelton Show"; "I Love Lucy"; Edward R. Murrow's "See It Now."*

New Products: *Power steering, by Chrysler Corporation; Tropicana products; sugarless chewing gum.*

The Academy Awards: *best picture—"An American in Paris"; best actor—Humphrey Bogart for "The African Queen"; best actress— Vivien Leigh for "A Streetcar Named Desire."*

1952

Puerto Rico *becomes an independent commonwealth of the U.S.*

British Overseas Airways *inaugurates the world's first commercial jet passenger service, with flights between London and Johannesburg.*

Bob Mathias *breaks his own decathlon record for an unprecedented second gold medal at the Summer Olympic Games in Helsinki.*

Richard M. Nixon, *Republican vice-presidential nominee, appears on national TV to deny accusations that he has used a secret slush fund to pay for personal expenses. He asserts that the only gift he has accepted from a constituent is Checkers, the family dog.*

The U.S. successfully tests *a hydrogen bomb on an atoll in the Marshall Islands.*

The price of a postcard stamp *rises from one cent to two cents.*

Bwana Devil, *the first feature-length 3-D movie, premieres. Special Polaroid glasses are required for viewing.*

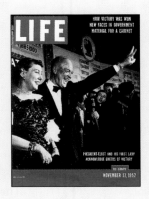

Dwight D. Eisenhower *is elected U.S. president, defeating Democratic candidate Adlai Stevenson.*

Army vet George Jorgensen, *26, travels to Copenhagen for the first sex change operation in medical history. He returns to the U.S. as Christine.*

New in Print: *"Mad" comic book; Norman Vincent Peale's "The Power of Positive Thinking"; Ralph Ellison's "Invisible Man."*

inspired trust and helped heal some of the political wounds from the Truman era. Vowing to take the nation on "the straight road down the middle," he created a benign climate for business. He stocked his cabinet with successful corporate leaders such as Secretary of Defense Charles Wilson, the former chief of General Motors, who summed up his own credo to a congressional committee: "What is good for the country is good for General Motors, and what's good for General Motors is good for the country." Ike's fiscal restraint kept prices stable, even holding the cost of first-class mail at three cents until 1958, when it rose a penny for the first time in 26 years.

In Ike's first year in office alone, the United States turned out two-thirds of all the world's manufactured goods. Unemployment dipped as low as 4.2 percent at mid-decade. The nation's output of goods and services rose by more than one-third during the '50s. Personal income doubled, and actual individual purchasing power jumped a whopping 30 percent.

Eisenhower could not claim credit for all or even most of the economic boom that was transforming American life. Like Ike himself, prosperity was largely a legacy of war. While laying waste to industry in Europe and Japan, World War II had left U.S. plants unscathed and vastly expanded. At the same time, priorities of war production had generated an immense pent-up demand for automobiles, household appliances, and other consumer goods.

Another result of the war, the GI Bill of Rights, augmented prosperity by creating an upwardly mobile generation of educated and ambitious veterans. Some 6.4 million veterans—nearly half of all who had served—took advantage of the GI Bill's generous aid to study in colleges, technical schools, or agricultural programs.

A Time to Buy: People had money in their pockets, and they were possessed by a ferocious urge to spend it. This was the beginning of the so-called consumer culture that encouraged Americans to purchase not merely to satisfy basic needs but to fulfill their fantasies of what constituted middle-class abundance. (Public opinion polls found that 3 in every 4 Americans thought of themselves as middle class.) In programs and commercials alike, television flashed constant images of such abundance. Largely because of TV, advertisers doubled their expenditures during the decade, imploring consumers to buy the latest-model car or appliance regardless of whether the old one had worn out. Easy credit made it possible. The first credit card, Diners Club, appeared in 1950, and ubiquitous installment plans—buy now,

New on TV: *"The Jackie Gleason Show"; "The Today Show"; "Dragnet"; "My Little Margie"; "The Adventures of Ozzie and Harriet."*

New Products: *Kellogg's Sugar Frosted Flakes; Kellogg's Sugar Smacks; paint-by-numbers kits; Sony pocket-sized transistor radio.*

The Academy Awards: *best picture—"The Greatest Show on Earth"; best actor—Gary Cooper for "High Noon"; best actress—Shirley Booth for "Come Back, Little Sheba."*

1953

Dwight D. Eisenhower *and Richard M. Nixon are inaugurated as president and vice president of the United States.*

Soviet Premier Joseph Stalin, *leader of the USSR since 1928, dies at the age of 72.*

Ernest Hemingway *wins the Pulitzer Prize for Fiction for "The Old Man and the Sea."*

Earl Warren, *governor of California, is appointed Chief Justice of the Supreme Court by President Eisenhower.*

Edmund Hillary and Tenzing Norgay reach the pinnacle of Mount Everest, over 29,000 feet above sea level.

Elizabeth II is crowned Queen of England in a coronation ceremony at Westminster Abbey, succeeding her late father King George VI.

Convicted in 1951 of espionage, Julius and Ethel Rosenberg are executed at Sing Sing Prison.

Ben Hogan becomes the first golfer to sweep the U.S. Open, the Masters, and the British Open in a single year.

Soviet Premier Georgi Malenkov announces that the Soviet Union has built a hydrogen bomb.

Senator John F. Kennedy marries former newspaper photographer Jacqueline Lee Bouvier.

Maureen Connelly, fondly known as "Litttle Mo" to her fans, becomes the first woman to win the Grand Slam in tennis by winning the Australian, French, English and U.S. women's singles titles.

The New York Yankees become the first team in baseball history to win five consecutive World Series.

An armistice ending the Korean War is signed at Panmunjom.

New in Print: "Playboy" magazine; "TV Guide"; Alfred Kinsey's "Sexual Behavior in the Human Female"; James Baldwin's "Go Tell It on the Mountain."

New on TV: "The Loretta Young Show"; "The Danny Thomas Show"; "The Life of Riley"; "You Are There"; "Name That Tune."

New Products: White Rose Redi-Tea, the first instant iced tea; the Corvette sports car.

The Academy Awards: best picture—"From Here to Eternity"; best actor—William Holden for "Stalag 17"; best actress—Audrey Hepburn for "Roman Holiday."

1954

The U.S. Navy launches Nautilus, its first nuclear-powered submarine.

Former Yankee center fielder Joe DiMaggio and movie star Marilyn Monroe marry; nine months later she files for divorce.

Mass inoculation against polio begins when schoolchildren in Pittsburgh receive the vaccine developed by Jonas E. Salk.

pay later—scorned the scrimping and saving that kept their parents and grandparents afloat during the Depression and wartime. As a result of the heady spending binge, personal indebtedness more than doubled.

The cornucopia of consumer goods for all was trumpeted to the world as the triumph of the American way over Communism. Appropriately, one of the most memorable peaceful confrontations between the United States and the Soviet Union took place in a state-of-the-art model kitchen at a trade exhibition in Moscow in 1959. Vice President Richard M. Nixon was escorting Soviet Premier Nikita Khrushchev through the American display when a heated argument erupted. The premier was in a belligerent mood because Washington had just issued its seventh annual Captive Nations Resolution and had appealed to Americans to pray for all people living in Communist regimes. When the vice president began bragging about the remote-controlled appliances, Khrushchev sneered, "Ha! These are mere gadgets! Don't you have a machine that puts food in the mouth and pushes it down?" Waving his finger angrily in Khrushchev's face, Nixon extolled the diversity of products and the right to choose that Western consumers enjoyed. The tension began to lift when a hostess in the kitchen turned on the household closed-circuit TV. Joked Khrushchev, "This is probably always out of order," and Nixon laughed and said in affirmation, "Da." The two leaders ended their "kitchen debate" with a friendly toast, and before Nixon headed for home the Russian accepted an invitation to make his first visit to the United States—a heartening sign of a Cold War thaw.

Parents Galore: A remarkable by-product of economic good times was the bumper crop of children born during the '50s. The baby boom, which actually began as early as 1943, peaked in 1957, when a record 4.3 million babies were born in the United States—one every seven seconds. Older couples who had delayed marriage and child-rearing because of the Depression and World War II felt they could at last afford children, and younger people enthusiastically plunged into domesticity. Americans were marrying younger—the average marriage age for women dropped to 20.1 years in 1956—and starting families sooner. "Of all the accomplishments of the American woman," announced *Life* magazine, "the one she brings off with the most spectacular success is having babies." The population spurted from 151.7 million in 1950 to 180.7 million in 1960, the largest 10-year increase in American history.

The baby boom proved to be a cause as well as a consequence of pros-

Four Puerto Rican nationalists *wound five members of Congress, firing from the visitors' gallery of the House of Representatives.*

The Army-McCarthy hearings *begin in Washington on April 22. They are broadcast on TV and run until June 17.*

Roger Bannister, *a British Medical student, breaks the four-minute barrier, running the mile in 3:59:4 at a track and field meet in Oxford, England.*

The French *are forced out of Vietnam, it's colony for 87 years, when Communist forces take the French fortress at Dienbienphu after a siege of 56 days.*

A Gallup poll *shows that a family of four can live on $60 a week.*

The Supreme Court, in a historic decision, unanimously overrules states rights and declares in Brown v. Board of Education of Topeka, Kansas that "in the field of public education the doctrine of 'separate but equal' has no place. Separate educational facilities are inherently unequal."

President Eisenhower signs legislation that changes the wording of the Pledge of Allegiance from "one nation, indivisible" to "one nation under God, indivisible."

Elvis Presley releases his first commercial recordings, "That's All Right" and "Blue Moon of Kentucky," on Sun Records.

The mambo, an African-Cuban dance with a sensual and exuberant beat, takes the country by storm, leading to hit records by artists like Perry Como and Cuban-born bandleader Perez "Prez" Prado.

The Miss America Pageant is first televised. Miss California, Lee Ann Meriwether, age 19, of San Francisco, is the winner.

The Defense Department announces the abolition of the last all-Negro units, completing the desegregation of the U.S. Armed Forces.

The silicon transistor is developed by Texas Instruments.

A report issued by the Tobacco Industry Research Committee states there is "no proof . . . that cigarette smoking is a cause of lung cancer."

The number of millionaires in the U.S. is reported to be 154.

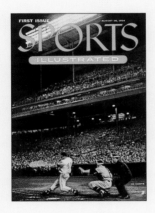

New in Print: "Sports Illustrated"; Bruce Catton's "A Stillness at Appomattox"; J. R. R. Tolkien's "The Lord of the Rings."

New Products: A. Swanson and Sons frozen TV dinners; Matchbox miniature cars; Con-Tact paper.

New on TV: "The Adventures of Rin Tin Tin"; "Caesar's Hour"; "Father Knows Best"; "Lassie"; "Tonight" with Steve Allen as host; "Disneyland."

The Academy Awards: best picture—"On the Waterfront"; best actor—Marlon Brando for "On the Waterfront"; best actress—Grace Kelly for "The Country Girl."

1955

Ray A. Kroc opens his first McDonald's restaurant in Des Plaines, Illinois.

Disc jockey Alan Freed hosts the first Rock 'n' Roll Party in New York City, featuring Fats Domino, The Drifters, Joe Turner, and the Moonglows.

Walt Disney Incorporated opens Disneyland, its $17 million amusement and entertainment park, in Anaheim, California.

perity. Youngsters needed diapers, machines to wash them, televisions to watch, and books to be raised by. Dr. Benjamin Spock's *The Common Sense Book of Baby and Child Care,* with its easygoing advice, sold more than one million copies a year—and raised the ire of older generations accustomed to sterner love. Baby boomers needed new schools, and California opened an average of a new one every week. "The baby boom symbolized a broader 'boom' mentality of many younger Americans," wrote historian James Patterson. "They were developing expectations that grew grander and grander over time."

Moving Up and Out: The prime expectation of most parents was a home of their own. Low interest rates and easy down payments under the GI Bill and the Federal Housing Administration made owning a house far more affordable. As young couples moved up, they moved out from the cities. Many went to suburban housing developments of the type pioneered in the potato fields of Long Island by William Levitt, an enterprising New York builder. In his first Levittown, a two-bedroom house sold for only $7,990. At that price, few complained about Levitt's rules. To keep the houses looking neat and similar, he required residents to mow their lawns once a week, banned fences, and—in those days before automatic dryers came into widespread use—forbade hanging the wash outside on weekends.

In 1950 alone, some 1.4 million single-family homes were built, most of them in the suburbs. By the end of the decade, one-fourth of all homes standing had been constructed during the '50s. Nearly 62 percent of the homes were owner-occupied, and one-third of all Americans lived in suburbia. Even *I Love Lucy* moved to the suburbs, relocating to Connecticut from New York City in 1956.

A Nation on Wheels: The necessary precondition for the growth of suburbia—and the linchpin of the economic boom—was the automobile *(pages 94-107)*. In 1955 Americans bought 7.9 million new automobiles, nearly four times as many as nine years before. Auto sales that year accounted for an astonishing one-fifth of the gross national product. The car, in its huge, high-finned incarnation of the day, not only shaped the suburban lifestyle but also brought the entire continent within reach of ordinary folks. In 1956 the Federal Aid Highway Act authorized the construction of 41,000 miles of interstate roads. A huge public-works project reminiscent of the New Deal,

Emmett Till, *14 (above with his mother, Mamie Bradley), is kidnapped, shot through the head, and mutilated because he supposedly whistled at a white woman while visiting in Money, Mississippi, from Chicago.*

President Eisenhower *suffers a mild heart attack. After a seven-week recuperation, he is back on the job.*

The Brooklyn Dodgers *beat the New York Yankees to win their first World Series ever.*

Using Ann Landers *as her pen name, Esther Pauline Friedman Lederer launches her advice column in the Chicago Sun-Times.*

Photographer Edward Steichen *mounts a 503-image exhibit, "The Family of Man," at the Museum of Modern Art in New York. A book follows later in the year.*

Rosa Parks *is arrested for refusing to give up her seat in the whites-only section of a bus in Montgomery, Alabama, touching off a yearlong boycott of the city's buses by blacks.*

George Meany *becomes president of the new union created by the merger of the American Federation of Labor and the Congress of Industrial Organizations.*

New in Print: *Sloan Wilson's "The Man in the Gray Flannel Suit."*

New on TV: *"Alfred Hitchcock Presents"; "Gunsmoke"; "The Honeymooners"; "The Lawrence Welk Show"; "The $64,000 Question"; "The Mickey Mouse Club"; "Mighty Mouse Playhouse," the first network animated series.*

New Products: *Rainbow Crafts' Play-Doh modeling compound; Ford Motors' Thunderbird; coonskin caps and other Davy Crockett-inspired merchandise for kids.*

The Academy Awards: *best picture—"Marty"; best actor—Ernest Borgnine for "Marty"; best actress—Anna Magnani for "The Rose Tattoo."*

1956

Tenley Albright *becomes the first American woman to win a gold medal in figure skating at the Winter Olympics in Cortina d'Ampezzo, Italy.*

The Supreme Court *extends the 1954 "Brown v. Board" decision to tax-supported colleges, banning segregation in all public institutions of higher learning.*

Roy Wilkins *becomes the third executive secretary of the National Association for the Advancement of Colored People (NAACP).*

Movie star Grace Kelly *abandons her career to wed Prince Rainier III of Monaco.*

The Federal Aid Highway Act *is passed by Congress, authorizing the construction of 41,000 miles of interstate highways.*

The Italian ocean liner *Andrea Doria sinks off Nantucket after colliding with the Swedish liner Stockholm. Five aboard the Stockholm and 52 on the Andrea Doria are killed.*

"In God We Trust" *becomes the motto of the United States and is added to new coins and currency.*

Dwight D. Eisenhower *is re-elected president.*

Floyd Patterson, *21, knocks out Archie Moore, 42, to become the youngest heavyweight champion in the history of the sport.*

Segregation *in public transportation is declared unconstitutional by the Supreme Court.*

New in Print: *Grace Metalious's "Peyton Place"; Allen Ginsberg's "Howl and Other Poems," published by fellow Beat poet and bookstore owner Lawrence Ferlinghetti.*

New on TV: *Dick Powell's "Zane Grey Theater"; "The Dinah Shore Chevy Show"; "Playhouse 90"; "The Nat King Cole Show."*

it was justified by the conservative Ike as necessary for national security.

Along this embryonic web of superhighways that would link every corner of the nation sprouted innovative enterprises such as motel chains. Holiday Inn, the first of the chains, was started in 1952 by Kemmons Wilson, a Memphis builder who had been enraged to find that every lodging place he stopped at charged extra for his five children. Fast-food restaurants proliferated, taking their cue from a former jazz pianist and milk-shake machine salesman named Ray Kroc. Intrigued by the assembly-line preparation of burgers, fries, and shakes developed by Dick and Maurice McDonald in California, Kroc took over their franchising operations. Then he bought them out, taking their name and transforming its first letter into the ubiquitous golden arches.

Motorists, paying 25 cents a gallon for gasoline on their way to new family entertainment centers such as California's Disneyland, gave little thought to the downside. Air pollution, the decline of trains and other public transit, the decay of the central city—no one paid much attention. Hardly anyone even noticed that over the course of the decade more Americans died in auto accidents than in all of World War II.

For many middle-class Americans—particularly men—the '50s would be the best decade of their lives. It was "a time of excitement and wonder," Ron Fimrite, a sportswriter, later noted of his halcyon days in San Francisco. "Late at night I would fall asleep to the reassuring moans of the foghorns on the bay. Tomorrow, I knew, would be rich with possibility."

Seeds of Change: Beneath the placid surface of mainstream optimism, however, bubbled deep currents of discontent and fear. Anxieties about the Cold War persisted, and they flared up with intensity at such times as the 1957 Soviet launching of *Sputnik I,* the first artificial satellite to orbit the earth *(pages 92-93). Sputnik* and its larger successors punctured U.S. complacency and posed the nightmare of nuclear warfare waged from outer space. The United States could and did reply with a determined technological effort, but more difficult challenges were taking shape at home.

Substantial sections of the nation did not share in the great expectations of the '50s. Most notably, these were African Americans, who made up nearly 11 percent of the population. Poverty afflicted at least half of black families, compared to a quarter of whites. And even more prosperous blacks were stymied in their pursuit of the American dream as they were excluded from many of the new housing developments. A few were able to break

New Products: *Comet cleanser; Crest toothpaste; Raid House & Garden Insecticide; Pampers disposable diapers; Burger King restaurant; Midas Muffler shop.*

The Academy Awards: *best picture—"Around the World in 80 Days"; best actor—Yul Brynner for "The King and I"; best actress— Ingrid Bergman for "Anastasia."*

1957

Martin Luther King Jr. *helps organize the Southern Christian Leadership Conference (SCLC) and becomes its first president.*

Evangelist Billy Graham *holds a five-month-long revival at Madison Square Garden in New York that attracts more than 500,000 people.*

Tennis player Althea Gibson *becomes the first black athlete to win at Wimbledon.*

The U.S. Congress *passes the first civil rights legislation since Reconstruction, establishing the Civil Rights Commission and a civil rights division in the attorney general's office.*

President Eisenhower *sends federal troops to Little Rock, Arkansas, to protect nine black students seeking to attend all-white Central High School.*

Conductor and composer *Leonard Bernstein becomes the first American-born music director of the New York Philharmonic.*

The Soviets *launch the first man-made satellite, Sputnik I, into orbit around earth.*

Sputnik II, *the Soviets' second satellite, is launched. Aboard is a dog named Laika, the first living creature in space.*

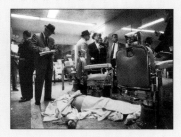

Mobster *Albert "The Executioner" Anastasia, whose Murder Inc. mob killed more than 60 rival racketeers in the '30s, is gunned down by two assassins while having his hair cut in a Manhattan barbershop.*

After 38 years, *Collier's magazine publishes its final issue.*

New in Print: *Dr. Seuss's "The Cat in the Hat"; Beat writer Jack Kerouac's "On the Road."*

New on TV: *"Have Gun Will Travel"; "American Bandstand" with Dick Clark; "Leave It to Beaver"; "Maverick"; "Perry Mason"; "The Price is Right"; "Wagon Train"; "Zorro."*

New Products: *Pink plastic flamingos; Wham-O's Pluto Platter, or Frisbee; Ford Motors' Edsel.*

The Academy Awards: *best picture—"The Bridge on the River Kwai"; best actor—Alec Guinness for "The Bridge on the River Kwai"; best actress—Joanne Woodward for "The Three Faces of Eve."*

1958

Jimmy Hoffa *is elected president of the International Brotherhood of Teamsters.*

The U.S. *launches its first satellite, Explorer I, into orbit around earth.*

The first National Library Week *is sponsored by the American Library Association and the National Book Committee.*

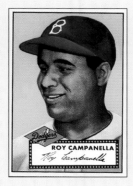

Roy Campanella *of the Brooklyn Dodgers, major league's first black catcher and three-time most valuable player, is paralyzed from the neck down in a car crash.*

Nikita Khrushchev *ousts Nikolai Bulganin and assumes leadership of the Communist Party and the government in the Soviet Union.*

National Airlines *inaugurates the first regular domestic jet service with flights between New York City and Miami.*

through the old barriers, however: Black and white members of the armed forces now served side by side thanks to President Truman's executive order of 1948, and black athletes like Bill Russell, Wilt Chamberlain, Hank Aaron, and Althea Gibson became champions in formerly all-white arenas.

Others struggled for equal rights in the courts and in the streets *(pages 108-121)*. After eight-year-old Linda Brown was turned away from her neighborhood school in Topeka, Kansas, the Supreme Court declared in 1954 in *Brown v. Board of Education of Topeka, Kansas* that separate school facilities were "inherently unequal." Three years after this landmark decision was handed down, President Eisenhower reluctantly sent troops to Central High School in Little Rock, Arkansas, to protect black students attempting to enroll. Meanwhile, Rosa Parks, a seamstress whose "feet hurt," refused to give up her seat on a bus in Montgomery, Alabama, to a white man. Her act spurred a boycott led by a young Baptist minister named Martin Luther King Jr.

Seeds of change were taking root in the white mainstream as well. Best-selling books such as *The Lonely Crowd* and *The Man in the Gray Flannel Suit* lashed out at the bland conformity of the new suburban culture. Allen Ginsberg, who belonged to a small movement of middle-class dropouts known as Beats, began his poem "Howl" with a haunting image: "I saw the best minds of my generation destroyed by madness, starving hysterical naked." Subversive possibilities lurked even in a young Memphis truck-driver's classic fulfillment of the American dream: Elvis Presley, in his pelvis-swiveling rise to rule the realm of rock and roll, spoke to the rebellious instincts of a new generation of youth.

Intimations of upheaval also stirred the provinces of sex and gender. A new report by biologist Alfred Kinsey, *Sexual Behavior in the Human Female,* shocked readers; Hugh Hefner's new magazine *Playboy* titillated them. Betty Friedan, a freelance magazine writer and suburban mother of three, discovered that many of her old Smith College classmates were frustrated and unfulfilled in traditional female roles. She distilled her findings—this "strange stirring, a sense of dissatisfaction, a yearning"—into an article called "Women Are People Too," which appeared in the September 1960 issue of *Good Housekeeping* magazine.

Even the redoubtable Lucy, it turned out, was not immune to the currents of discontent. Lucille Ball divorced Desi Arnaz in 1960, three years after the 179th and final new episode of *I Love Lucy* had aired. Both the show and the decade had had a good run. Now more turbulent times lay ahead.

Van Cliburn *becomes the first American to win the prestigious International Tchaikovsky Piano Competition in Moscow.*

The San Francisco Giants, *with Willie Mays, and the Los Angeles Dodgers play their first game as west coast teams after moving from New York.*

The National Aeronautics and Space Administration (NASA) *is established to direct nonmilitary space activities.*

Pope Pius XII *dies at the age of 82. Nineteen days later, a new pontiff, Pope John XXIII, is elected.*

The Federal Aviation Agency (FAA) *is established to control civilian and military air traffic.*

New in Print: *John Kenneth Galbraith's "The Affluent Society"; Truman Capote's "Breakfast at Tiffany's."*

New on TV: *"The Donna Reed Show"; "The Garry Moore Show"; "Peter Gunn"; "77 Sunset Strip."*

New Products: *Sweet 'n Low; the American Express credit card; the Bic pen; Wham-O's Hula Hoop; the first Pizza Hut.*

The Academy Awards: *best picture—"Gigi"; best actor—David Niven for "Separate Tables"; best actress—Susan Hayward for "I Want to Live!"*

1959

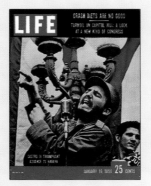

Guerrilla forces *led by Fidel Castro overthrow Cuban dictator Fulgencio Batista on New Year's Day.*

Rock and rollers *Buddy Holly ("That'll Be the Day"), Ritchie Valens ("La Bamba"), and "The Big Bopper" a.k.a. J. P. Richardson ("Chantilly Lace") die when their tour plane crashes near Clear Lake, Iowa.*

Alaska and Hawaii *become the 49th and 50th states to enter the Union.*

In a model kitchen *at the American National Exhibition in Moscow, Vice President Richard Nixon and Nikita Khrushchev argue about capitalism and communism in what comes to be called their "kitchen debate."*

British anthropologist *Louis S. B. Leakey discovers 1.75 million-year-old skull fragments of an ancestral hominoid, Zinjanthropus boisei, in the Olduvai Gorge in Tanganyika.*

Berry Gordy Jr. *founds Tamla Records, later to become Motown Records, in Detroit.*

The Solomon R. Guggenheim Museum, *designed by Frank Lloyd Wright, opens in New York City.*

NASA *names the first astronauts. Pictured from left to right, front row: Walter Schirra, Donald Slayton, John Glenn, and Scott Carpenter. Back row: Alan Shepard, Virgil Grissom, and Gordon Cooper.*

New in Print: *Philip Roth's "Goodbye, Columbus"; James Michener's "Hawaii."*

New on TV: *"Bat Masterson"; "Bonanza"; "Dennis the Menace"; "The Twilight Zone"; "The Untouchables."*

New Products: *Mattel's Barbie doll; Mead Johnson Company's Metracal diet drink; General Mills' Frosty Os; pantyhose stockings.*

The Academy Awards: *best picture—"Ben-Hur"; best actor—Charlton Heston for "Ben-Hur"; best actress—Simone Signoret for "Room at the Top."*

Icons of
an Era

★

Although one cynic called the Eisenhower years a case of "the bland leading the bland," the 1950s were rich with remarkable personalities. A Baptist minister, Martin Luther King Jr., led a bus boycott in Alabama and emerged as spokesman of the burgeoning civil rights movement. World War II hero Douglas MacArthur reversed the course of the war in Korea, only to lose his job after making rash public comments disputing the president's war aims. In Hollywood, the young actor James Dean, star of *Rebel Without a Cause*, became a symbol of frustrated youth even as he hurtled toward untimely death.

A movie star who glowed even more brightly was Marilyn Monroe (37-23-37), the decade's premier sex symbol. Monroe received 5,000 fan letters a week. When she visited Japan, people fell into fishponds to get a glimpse of the *shiri-furi* (buttock-swinging) actress. On-screen, her characters were usually fluffy-headed lightweights; off-screen, she was a complex, often unhappy young woman, obsessed with becoming a serious actress and uncomfortable with a public image that had become almost impossible to control.

Poorly equipped to handle the pressures of celebrity, Monroe had a touching vulnerability that, ironically, only added to her appeal. "Sometimes [fame] makes you a little bit sad because you'd like to meet somebody kind of on face value," she once commented. "It's nice to be included in people's fantasies, but you also like to be accepted for your own sake."

The curves, blond hair, and enigmatic pout were part of Marilyn Monroe's glamorous yet wistful appeal. Combined with her comedic talent in such films as Some Like It Hot, they made her an American legend.

I believe we must try to limit the war to Korea for these vital reasons: to make sure that the precious lives of our fighting men are not wasted; to see that the security of our country and the free world is not needlessly jeopardized; and to prevent a third world war. A number of events have made it evident that General MacArthur did not agree with that policy. I have therefore considered it essential to relieve General MacArthur so that there would be no doubt or confusion as to the real purpose and aim of our policy.
—President Harry S. Truman

When you put on a uniform, there are certain inhibitions which you accept.
—General Dwight D. Eisenhower

In the opinion of the Joint Chiefs, [MacArthur's] strategy would involve us in the wrong war, at the wrong place, at the wrong time and with the wrong enemy.
—General Omar Bradley

His dismissal by the President is the culmination of disastrous failure of leadership in Washington.
—Governor Thomas E. Dewey, New York

If MacArthur had his way, not one Asian would have believed the U.S. has a civilian government.
—Socialist Norman Thomas

I do not think a general should make policies.
—Eleanor Roosevelt

Our only choice is to impeach President Truman.
—Senator William Jenner, Indiana

President Truman has given [the Communists] just what they were after—MacArthur's scalp.
—Senator Richard M. Nixon, California

American Caesar

Imperious, theatrical, brilliant, General Douglas MacArthur was not a man who invited neutrality: Some worshiped him, some loathed him. During his glory days as supreme Allied commander in the Pacific during World War II, most worshiped him. After a stellar wartime record, it was MacArthur who accepted Japan's surrender in Tokyo Bay and went on to rule the defeated island nation during its lengthy postwar occupation.

West Point to his core, MacArthur was the son of another general—"the most flamboyantly egotistical man I had ever seen," one of the father's aides said, "until I met his son." Overconfidence that many called arrogance would ultimately prove to be MacArthur's fatal flaw. In June of 1950, after North Korean troops invaded South Korea, MacArthur was named commander of the United Nations forces protecting the South. At first he succeeded, reversing seemingly certain defeat. Then, 10 months later, President Harry Truman fired him for publicly flouting U.S. policy by advocating the bombing and blockading of Communist China.

A shocked and emotional nation divided into two camps, for MacArthur and against him. Supporters seemed to be in the majority; the five-star general arrived home to be besieged by adoring crowds wherever he went. Millions watched on television as their hero—as great on a podium as on a battlefield—addressed Congress. "Old soldiers never die," he intoned, "they just fade away. And like the old soldier of that ballad, I now close my military career and just fade away—an old soldier who tried to do his duty as God gave him the light to see that duty. Goodbye."

Despite a swell of support for him to run for president, MacArthur decided to fade into the board of directors of Sperry-Rand. Meanwhile, military experts denounced MacArthur's views as reckless at a Senate hearing that confirmed Truman's position: The military is supposed to implement policy, not make it.

Snapping out orders during his brilliant amphibious assault on Inchon Harbor, General MacArthur reaches his high point as U.N. commander in Korea.

I don't make promises that a bottle of ointment will cure you of everything from poverty to flat feet.
—First presidential campaign, July 1952

A people that values its privileges above its principles soon loses both.
—First inaugural address, January 20, 1953

My first day at the president's desk. Plenty of worries and difficult problems. But such has been my portion for a long time—the result is that this just seems (today) like a continuation of all I've been doing since July 1941—even before that.
—Diary entry, January 21, 1953

The only way to win World War III is to prevent it.
—Radio and TV address, September 19, 1956

The final battle against intolerance is to be fought—not in the chambers of any legislature—but in the hearts of men.
—Second presidential campaign, October 1956

The spirit of our people is the strength of our nation. Strength is not just in arms and guns and planes: it's not just in factories and in fertile farms. It's in the heart, the heart that venerates the heritage we have from our fathers, the heritage of freedom, of self-government. That is the basic strength of America.
—Victory speech, election night, November 6, 1956

We seek peace. And now as in no other age, we seek it because we have been warned, by the power of modern weapons, that peace may be the only climate possible for human life itself. Yet this peace we seek cannot be born of fear alone. There must be justice, sensed and shared by all peoples.
—Second inaugural address, January 21, 1957

I Like Ike!

Affable, folksy, and a war hero, Dwight David Eisenhower was a slogan writer's dream. "Make the White House a Dwight House" was one motto of his 1952 run for president. Then there was "Peace and Power with Eisenhower," and the enormously effective "I Like Ike." It was no surprise that enough Americans did like Ike to give him landslide victories over Democratic rival Adlai Stevenson in 1952 and again in 1956. Supreme commander of the Allied Expeditionary Force in Europe in World War II, Eisenhower was a national institution long before he ran for office, a respected leader whose infectious grin was said in his war years to be worth 10 divisions. As a rueful Stevenson once admitted, "I like Ike, too."

Despite the charm, some postwar pundits thought he lacked the intellectual armament to be a successful candidate—or an effective president. Those who saw past the rosy facade knew better, sensing a shrewdness, toughness, and ambition that Ike took some pains to conceal. He proved a thoroughly savvy campaigner, using advertising as no candidate had before, and harnessing the growing power of television to take his famous grin into millions of American homes. The smile, and the apparent sincerity behind it, reassured a nation emerging from two decades of Depression and war.

Critics complained that as president Eisenhower was backward on civil rights and other social issues and that he seemed to prefer golfing to governing. But he was a man for his hour in history, and most Americans loved him.

"The popularity of President Eisenhower has got beyond the bounds of reasonable calculation and will have to be put down as a national phenomenon, like baseball. The thing is no longer a remarkable political fact but a kind of national love affair," wrote the *New York Times*'s James Reston, who saw the president as the perfect embodiment of Americans in the 1950s. "What America is at this moment of her history," Reston concluded, "so is Eisenhower."

Eisenhower greets admirers during a 1952 campaign stop in Springfield, Illinois. His appeal reached across party lines to attract many traditional Democrats.

Troubled Genius

An erudite man who once learned to read Sanskrit as a hobby, physicist J. Robert Oppenheimer entered the 1950s a hero for his work in leading the scientific team that developed the atomic bomb during World War II. Three years later, his character was cast in doubt by witch-hunting bureaucrats caught up in the era's Red-baiting frenzy *(pages 76-81)*. After lengthy hearings by a three-man panel of the Atomic Energy Commission (AEC), he was declared a security risk—not for disloyalty to his country but for such perfectly legal proclivities as having Communist friends and "lacking enthusiasm" for developing the still more powerful hydrogen bomb. The AEC then fired Oppenheimer as a consultant, to the outrage of concerned journalists and much of the scientific community, who saw the case as a clear assault on intellectual inquiry and free speech.

The great majority of this country's leading physicists harbored the most profound doubts about the wisdom of making a vast investment in the hydrogen project. These doubts were in part moral. And why should they not be, since physicists are also human beings? . . . But the point is that the physicists had a right to be wrong. . . . This right—the privilege of making an honest error of judgment without being labeled a traitor—is basic to free science and a free society.

—Joseph and Stewart Alsop, *Washington Post*

As citizens and scientists, we are deeply disturbed. . . . Our concern is not so much with Dr. Oppenheimer as an individual, honored and respected as he is by us, as with the larger considerations of the apparent change in the government security policy. . . . If the consequences to the individual of an unpopular or unwise decision are the same as the consequences of a disloyal act, then the making of decisions or the taking of responsibility for vital programs will be shunned, and two important ingredients of national strength—faith in the individual's honesty of judgment and willingness to back one's opinions with action—will become increasingly rare.

—Statement signed by 214 scientists

Fired from government service as a security risk, atomic scientist J. Robert Oppenheimer became a symbol of both repressed freedom and scientific morality.

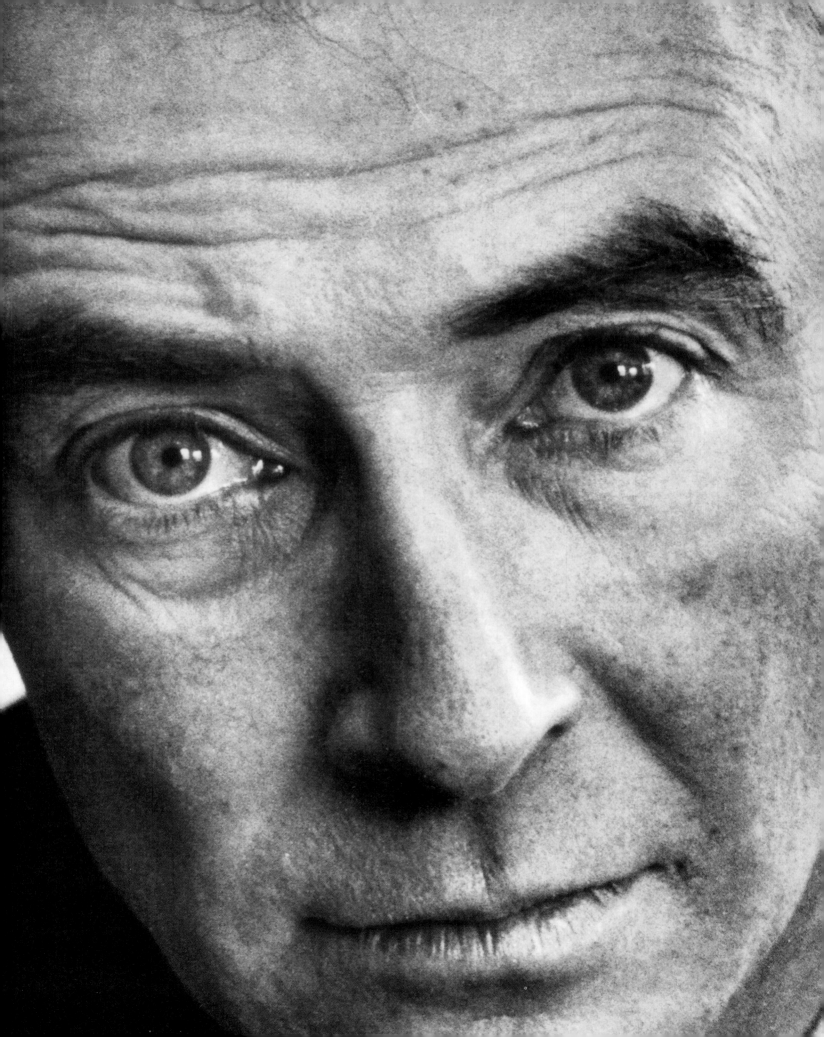

A Glowing Union

She brought to the marriage style, breeding, elegance. He brought brilliance, verve, ambition. Their wedding in Newport, Rhode Island, on September 12, 1953, was the social event of the decade.

Outside the church, 3,000 onlookers mobbed the bride before the ceremony. Inside, some 700 prominent guests later saw an unruffled Jacqueline Lee Bouvier, 24, sweep down the aisle in 50 yards of ivory silk taffeta toward her groom, 36-year-old Massachusetts senator John Fitzgerald Kennedy.

It was "just like a coronation," said a guest—a remark that seemed prophetic later in the decade as Kennedy energetically sought the presidency with Jackie at his side.

I was already a successful politician when we were married so she at first felt she wasn't necessary to my career. Now that we have started out on a new and far more massive operation she is much more interested. . . . She breathes all of the political gases that flow around us, but she never seems to inhale them.
—Presidential candidate John F. Kennedy, August 1959

At their wedding reception, Jacqueline Kennedy adjusts her bridal finery while her new husband begins his lunch.

On protest . . .

Nonviolence is the most potent technique for oppressed people. Unearned suffering is redemptive.

On voting rights . . .

All types of conniving methods are still being used to prevent Negroes from becoming registered voters. The denial of this right is a betrayal of the highest mandates of our democratic traditions. So our most urgent request to the President of the United States and every member of Congress is to give us the right to vote. . . . Give us the ballot and we will fill the legislative halls with men of good will. Give us the ballot and we will place judges on the benches of the South who will do justly and love mercy and we will place at the head of the southern states governors who have felt not only the tang of the human but also the glow of the divine.

On hate . . .

If we are arrested every day, if we are exploited every day, if we are trampled over every day, don't ever let anyone pull you so low as to hate. There is an element of God in every man.

On segregation . . .

Many unconsciously wondered whether they deserved better conditions. Their minds were so conditioned to segregation that they submissively adjusted to things as they were. This is the ultimate tragedy of segregation. It not only harms one physically but injures one spiritually.

On civil disobedience . . .

I was proud of my crime. It was the crime of joining my people in a nonviolent protest against injustice. . . . It was the crime of desiring for my people the unalienable rights of life, liberty, and the pursuit of happiness. It was above all the crime of seeking to convince my people that noncooperation with evil is just as much a moral duty as cooperation with good.

The Apostle of Nonviolence

The Reverend Martin Luther King Jr., a scholarly young man, had studied the tactics of nonviolence and of passive resistance to unjust laws. He came to believe that those strategies could actually set in motion a shift of conscience in America, a slow but certain move toward racial justice. "Christian love can bring brotherhood on earth," he preached. "There is an element of God in every man. No matter how low one sinks into racial bigotry, he can be redeemed."

King was an inexperienced 26-year-old when, in 1955, he found himself leading a black boycott of Montgomery, Alabama's, segregated buses *(pages 114-117).* The oldest son of an Atlanta minister, he had previously led a relatively sheltered life; the boycott was his first experience of real adversity. King later recalled sitting at the kitchen table one night in despair after receiving one of many telephoned threats—only to have a powerful religious experience. "It seemed at that moment," he said, "that I could hear an inner voice saying to me, 'Martin Luther, stand up for righteousness. Stand up for justice. Stand up for truth. And lo I will be with you, even until the end of the world.' "

Buttressed by his renewed faith, King did not waver even when three days later, his home was bombed. Then and ever afterward, he was committed to meet violence with nonviolence, having faith that hate must wither in the face of implacable love. "The strong man," he said, "is the man who can stand up for his rights and not hit back."

Over time, that message galvanized a movement that would spread from the South throughout the country. Its simple heroism would become King's lasting legacy to those seeking social justice: The courage to resist, the power to love, the strength to endure.

Preaching the powerful faith of forgiveness, Dr. Martin Luther King Jr. gave the civil rights movement a new, nationwide impetus in the 1950s.

The Rebel

On-screen and in life he was the smoldering loner, tough but vulnerable, dangerous, beautiful, and lost, the outsider everybody wanted to let in. James Dean, 24, was killed instantly on September 30, 1955, in a car crash at nightfall on a California highway. Gone, he left behind only three films—*East of Eden, Rebel Without a Cause,* and *Giant*—to mark his brief and burning trajectory. As suggested in the poem below by novelist John Dos Passos, however, dying young rendered Dean's youth imperishable. In life, he was just becoming a star. Dead, he became a legend.

There is nothing much deader
than a dead motion picture actor, and yet,
even after James Dean had been some years dead,
*   when they filed out of the close darkness*
and the breathedout air of the second and third
and fourth run motion picture theatres
where they'd been seeing James Dean's old films,
they still lined up:
*   the boys in the jackboots and the leather jackets,*
the boys in the skintight jeans, the boys in broad
motorbike belts, before the mirrors in the restroom
to look at themselves and see James Dean;
*   the resentful hair, the deep eyes*
floating in lonesomeness, the bitter beat look,
the scorn on the lip. . . .
*   The girls flocked out dizzy with wanting*
to run their fingers through his hair,
to feel that thwarted maleness; girl-boy almost,
but he needs a shave . . .
"Just him and me in the back seat of a car."
*   Their fathers snort, but sometimes they remember:*
"Nobody understood me either. I might have amounted
to something if the folks had understood."
The older women struggle from their seats weteyed.

Sad, bad James Dean, the '50s' icon of wayward youth, had a taciturn appeal that won him the ultimate teenage accolade: "Everything he said was cool."

The Princess

In the decade of moviedom's blonde bombshell, Grace Kelly was something altogether different: the epitome of aloof allure and subtle, silken sensuality. The willowy daughter of a prominent Philadelphia family, Kelly appeared in her first small film part in 1951 at the age of 21. A year later, she played a strait-laced Quaker bride to Gary Cooper's sheriff in *High Noon,* and the next year almost won an Oscar for her role as an upper-class English-woman opposite Clark Gable in *Mogambo.*

That nomination brought her to the attention of director Alfred Hitchcock, and the most fruitful connection of her career. "I didn't discover Grace," Hitchcock once said, "but I saved her from a fate worse than death. I prevented her from being eternally cast as a cold woman." Moviegoers were charmed and bewitched by Kelly's work in three Hitchcock films in two years—*Dial M for Murder* and *Rear Window* in 1954, and *To Catch a Thief* in 1955.

With a brand-new studio contract and at the zenith of her popularity as a movie star, Kelly gave it all up for the permanent role of Her Serene Highness Princess Grace of Monaco, wife of Prince Rainier III of the House of Grimaldi, Europe's oldest ruling dynasty. Her fiancé's domain, a 370-acre principality with a casino-based economy, was perhaps not quite as impressive as his title, but their April 19, 1956, wedding was a worldwide sensation, with Grace drenchingly lovely in a gown trailed by a 10-foot train of lace. Later that day, in the perfect end to a fairy-tale romance, an airplane showered the young couple's honeymoon yacht with 15,000 carnations.

Grace met him when she was on the French Riviera. She went there to make a picture called To Catch a Thief—and look what she came back with.
—John B. "Jack" Kelly, father of the bride, 1956

In the royal palace in Monte Carlo, Grace Kelly pauses for a private moment as she prepares to become princess of tiny but terribly chic Monaco.

Detroit autoworker Darwin Smith and his family were as pleased as punch with their new house and a Ford coupe to go with it.

Living the Good Life

★

IN THE SUBURBAN PROMISED LAND

Streamwood, Elmwood, Cedar Hill, Cockrell Hill, Park Forest, Deer Park. The very names of America's fresh-minted postwar suburbs evoked visions of tree-dotted meadows, rolling hills, and shadowy forests. The reality—grids of tidy little clapboard houses on grassy plots dotted with skinny saplings and some knee-high shrubs—didn't quite square with such visions. Nevertheless, battalions of veterans and former war workers and young married couples, many aided by the GI bill and federally subsidized mortgages, streamed out of the cities to stake out their claims to a new way of life.

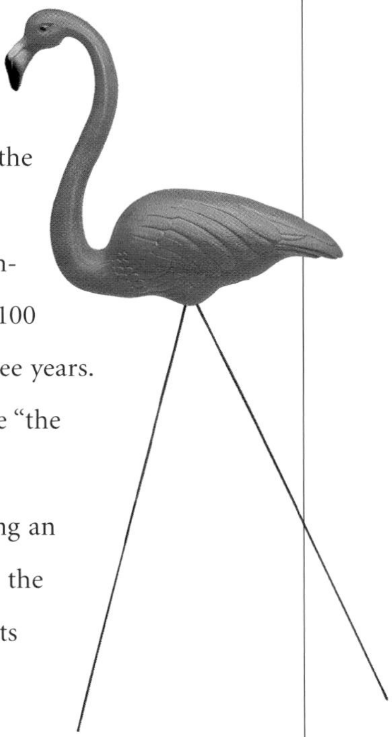

It was a bonanza for builders, who added new housing at an astonishing rate. In the California suburb of Lakewood, for example, as many as 100 houses were started each day, and 17,500 were completed in less than three years. By 1955, *House and Garden* magazine reported that suburbia had become "the national way of life."

With paychecks fatter than ever—the average suburbanite was earning an estimated $6,500 by 1954—and an equally great fund of optimism about the future, the burgeoning young middle class happily kicked the frugal habits of the Depression and the war years and went on a buying spree. Filling their nests with a dazzling array of goods from power lawn mowers and hi-fi's to pink flamingos and martini glasses, they and their broods of children settled down to enjoy the good life, suburban style.

The Men in the Gray Flannel Suits

Sloan Wilson, author of the classic '50s novel *The Man in the Gray Flannel Suit,* experienced suburban life firsthand when he lived with his family in New Canaan, Connecticut. Five days a week he traveled to and from Manhattan by train with a horde of other aspiring young professionals. Wilson and his fellow commuters, all dressed in drab-colored, uniform-like suits "looked like soldiers as we lined up to climb aboard the trains . . . which reminded me of troop carriers." Once in town, after toiling 10 or 12 hours to finance their family's upscale lifestyle, at the end of the day the weary army boarded the train for home.

The commuting lifestyle was fodder for cartoonists *(above, right)* and for intellectuals who declared that it helped breed mindless conformity. But the average suburban man ignored such jabs and concentrated on advancing his career. According to one observer's recollection, the prospects for success were excellent: "If you had a college diploma, a dark suit, and anything between the ears, it was like an escalator; you just stood there and you moved up."

Commuters	1950	1960
Commuter Railroads	46	30
Rail Commuter Passenger Rides *millions*	277	203
New York City Auto Commuters *thousands*	640 *est.*	866

Railroads cut service just as the number of commuters grew (above). More and more of them turned to cars, as shown above for New York.

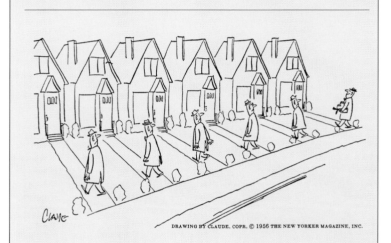

DRAWING BY CLAUDE. COPR. © 1956 THE NEW YORKER MAGAZINE, INC.

On a January evening in 1958, commuters on a New York Central train catch up on the news. Many regulars habitually commandeered seats facing each other for their nightly card games.

"We looked like soldiers as we lined up to climb aboard . . ."

Sloan Wilson

Homeward-bound commuters in look-alike hats and overcoats arrive in Park Forest, Illinois, outside Chicago. At upper right, a man dashing for his train clutches a briefcase. Many commuters felt undressed without one, even though it often contained nothing more than a newspaper.

"Atom" clock

Cloverleaf table

Porcelain duck

Pitcher

Feathering the Nest

Do-it-yourself decorators went all out to create a personal look in houses barely distinguishable from one another on the outside. But the desire for individuality was at war with conformist impulses: "Everybody had to have the same things everybody else had," one housewife commented. Tupperware, for instance, was in practically every kitchen, and neighbors

A Tupperware party (above) gave housewives an opportunity to socialize and to

took the trading stamps *(right, top)* that local supermarkets and service stations gave them to the same showroom to swap for furniture and accessories.

Style-setting suburban sophisticates liked the "organic" modern look of curvy tables and molded plastic chairs *(right, bottom)*. Just as up-to-date were items inspired by science, such as the "atom" clock opposite, and the arty crowd used fabrics, Formica, and vinyl flooring patterned with squiggly lines recalling Jackson Pollock's abstract paintings *(pages 134-135)*.

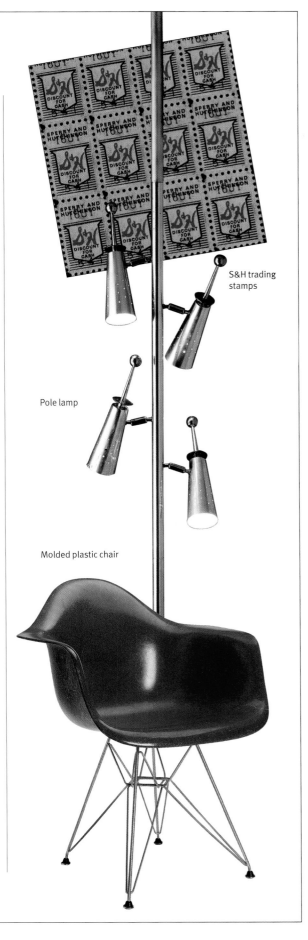

S&H trading stamps

Pole lamp

Molded plastic chair

buy the latest items in the popular line of plasticware.

Cooking Sure to Please the Family

Advertisements pictured the ideal woman of the '50s as a cheery homemaker in a crisp, frilly apron, finding her deepest satisfaction and joy in cooking for her family.

"Good things baked in the kitchen will keep romance far longer than bright lipstick," pronounced Marjorie Husted, creator of Betty Crocker, a prime female icon of the '50s. It was a message women of the day could hardly miss. Television, radio, and magazines bombarded them with the assurance that the kitchen was their realm and that loving food preparation for their families was the way to fulfillment.

The companion message was that the lucky woman whose husband could provide a middle-class life in the suburbs would eagerly abandon any career aspirations. A wife's job, as defined by the popular *House Beautiful,* was to meet her husband's every need, "understanding why he wants it this way, forgetting your own preferences." He was, the magazine asserted, "the boss." However, the wife wasn't to regard herself as subservient. Indeed, *Time* magazine called her "the key figure in all suburbia . . . the keeper of the suburban dream."

Women who plunged into the stay-at-home role were a perfect target audience for food manufacturers pushing new timesaving "heat and serve," "quick 'n' easy" dishes that could be prepared "in a jiffy." Colorful images of Velveeta treats and molded Jell-O salads and aspics *(below)* marched across magazine pages. And the image of the aproned housewife beaming at her mastery of yet another man-pleasing recipe was ubiquitous.

Miracle Mixes

Magazines of the 1950s were filled with color advertisements that promoted easy recipes and tempted women to trade in cooked-from-scratch traditional fare for modern meals whipped up with the contents of a box or can.

Party Time

Many couples transplanted to suburbia felt lonely and craved a sense of community. One response to this problem was the neighborhood cocktail party *(right)*, which became a ritual weekend event. Writer Sloan Wilson observed that in New Canaan, Connecticut, "a good many people regarded the thought of a mailbox without invitations as a calamity. . . ." Despite their forced gaiety, cocktail parties did allow people to get acquainted with their neighbors, and anyone who received an invitation could view it as a reassuring sign that he was in the swim socially.

Ronson lighter *(above)*

Matched set of bar glasses *(below)*

Drinks Anyone?	1950	1960
Gin production *millions of gallons*	6	19
Vodka production *millions of gallons*	0.1 *est.*	9
Aspirin sales *millions of pounds*	12	18

"Oh, oh, they've got the dictionary out. It's going to be one of THOSE evenings!"

Liquor production and aspirin sales shot up during the decade of the cocktail party (chart, top), which often featured party games as well as drinking (cartoon, above). Cocktail glasses like those above and at far left also sold briskly during this time.

A four-year-old proudly sports a coonskin cap and Davy Crockett shirt. A three-part television series about the legendary woodsman launched a craze that gripped the younger set in 1955.

Lionel Train

A Toy Chest Full of Childhood Fun

Conceived for children (and vice versa), suburbia was a wonderland of toys. The parents of postwar babies had grown up in leaner times, and they wanted their kids to have what they'd missed out on themselves. On holidays and birthdays and lots of occasions in between, these indulgent moms and dads showered their children with toys and board games, bicycles and books.

Perennial favorites like sleds, Erector Sets, baby dolls, Lincoln Logs, toy cars, model trains, and jump ropes were more popular than ever. Modern technology also yielded some brand-new items. One such was Silly Putty, concocted during a wartime search for synthetic substitutes for rubber. The bouncy blob was no help in the war effort, but it was an instant success when it went on the market in 1950. Mr. Potato Head, the man of a thousand funny faces, came on the scene a couple of years later. The first toy ever advertised on TV, he came packaged as a collection of 28 molded plastic pieces—body, face parts, a pipe, and other accessories— to stick into a plain old potato from mom's vegetable bin. These best-loved toys—and many more that made childhood fun in the '50s—are pictured here and on the following pages.

Skipping to a rhythmic ditty, a girl with bouncing curls demonstrates her best rope-jumping form, unimpeded by her full-skirted dress and best shoes. Jumping rope was largely a female amusement, along with jacks and hopscotch.

Army truck

Comic book

Play-Doh

View-Master with reel

In 1958, the Hula Hoop fad kept 30 million Americans twirling away. Some kids could keep as many as five hoops going at once.

Electronic football game

Flexible Flyer sled

Marbles

Eloise book

Dr. Seuss book

Tonka pickup truck

Erector Set

Mr. Potato Head

Comic book

Antiaircraft truck

Comic books

Lincoln Logs

Whooping and brandishing cap-firing rifles, gleeful boys in New Jersey reenact the last battle and death of the coonskin-capped King of the Wild Frontier.

Water pistol

Miniature cars

Schwinn Black Phantom bicycle

Comic book

Silly Putty

Toy kitchen

Tiny Tears doll

Teen Fun and Games

L ike their parents, teenagers in the '50s were a conformist lot, at least on the surface. A few marched boldly to their own drummer, but the majority did their best to dress like everyone else, to have dates for football games and dances, to cruise around town with a carload of friends. The aim was to seem normal—and never to be called "square." Girls had an added worry: their reputation. They didn't want people to say they were "fast," and they took to heart the warning a Princeton undergraduate delivered in a *Seventeen* magazine advice column: If a girl kissed him goodnight on the first date, he wrote, "I can't help thinking about how many others there may have been."

In fact, dating around—and kissing lots of boys—was the exception. Most kids went steady, and not always strictly for love. As one practical young woman remarked, "If you go around with a boy for a while, no one else asks you for dates, so why not go steady?"

"Fresh up" with Seven-Up!

Beneath the thumping feet of a pompom-wielding squad of cheerleaders, players on a Seattle football team await their chance to get off the bench and into the action (right). Rivalry between high schools was fierce, and pep rallies the night before a game whipped school spirit up to a fever pitch.

A couple sways dreamily to a slow tune (above) at a party in 1954. A mainstay of teenage social life, dances often took place on Friday nights in the school gym or cafeteria. A portable record player like the one shown here was a fixture at teenage parties.

All the Rage

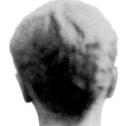

The '50s fashion plate was all curves, thanks to French couturier Christian Dior, whose "New Look" took America by storm. "I turned them into flowers," Dior said, "with soft shoulders, blooming bosoms, waists slim as vine stems, and skirts opening up like blossoms." Women not endowed with a blooming bosom made padded bra sales soar. In pursuit of the hourglass ideal, they wore their bodices snug and buoyed up their full, below-the-calf skirts with flouncy petticoats. Also the rage were strapless dresses and swimsuits, eye-popping short shorts, and poodle motifs (right and opposite).

Men had a New Look of their own. Some dared to wear Bermuda shorts to work in summer (above). On weekends, they shed their dull workaday clothes for splashy sport shirts and slacks in sizzling reds, pinks, and yellows. Such gorgeous plumage, a 1952 Arrow shirt ad declared, would put romance into a fellow's "loaf life."

A Lot of Leg

In the summer of 1956, a willowy young woman photographed on a Detroit street corner pauses to tug her scanty shorts down a little (right). Most communities, including Detroit, were open-minded about the display of so much skin in public places. However, in White Plains, N.Y., and a few other towns, the police handed out summonses to women caught wearing short shorts, which were deemed violations of local ordinances governing proper attire for ladies.

Handbag with bas-relief poodle design

Silk dress with built-in petticoat

Life magazine praised circle skirts as "ideal for home entertaining because their big, novel patterns become immediate conversation pieces."

Two shorts-clad friends go shopping for crinolines. For maximum effect, some teenagers starched petticoats so heavily that they stood up on their own.

In the Pink

Pink—blush pink, rose pink, cherry pink, shocking pink— was the color of the '50s. A faint rosy glow was on the horizon when the decade dawned: In 1949, Brooks Brothers, purveyor of clothes to staid Ivy Leaguers, introduced a pale pink button-down oxford-cloth dress shirt. It lent a little pizazz to the sober gray-flannel suit, as did suspenders and neckties in subtle tints. For men with flashier tastes, there were shocking pink sports coats, suits, and slacks. Teenage boys emulating Elvis Presley's style wore black pegged pants with a pink stripe down the side seam.

Women's fashion took a cue from pink-loving First Lady Mamie Eisenhower's wardrobe, and decorators borrowed the hue of boudoir and powder room for living rooms and kitchens. At the peak of the craze practically anything the consumer could desire could be had in roseate tones, from appliances to plumbing fixtures to cars and toilet tissue—that ultimate touch in color coordination.

In front of his Harlem café, colorfully clothed prizefighter Sugar Ray Robinson leans on his 1950 Cadillac (far right), which was custom-painted to match his favorite necktie.

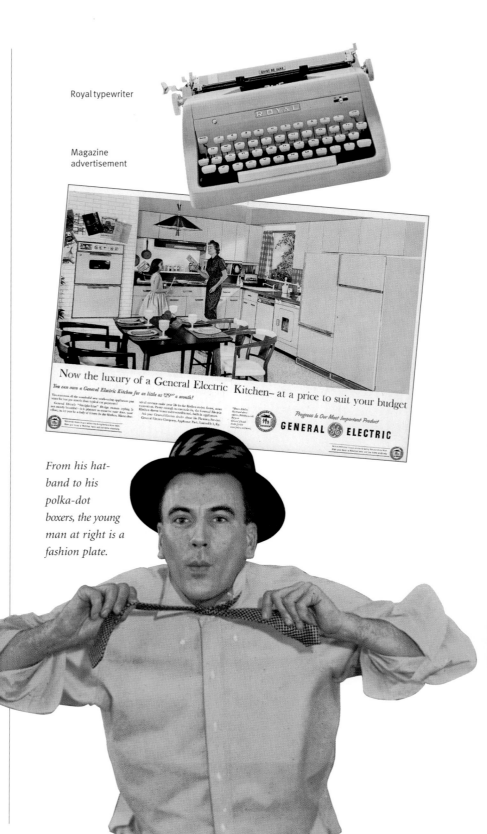

Royal typewriter

Magazine advertisement

Now the luxury of a General Electric Kitchen– at a price to suit your budget

Progress Is Our Most Important Product

GENERAL ELECTRIC

From his hat-band to his polka-dot boxers, the young man at right is a fashion plate.

The Red Threat

★

THE COLD WAR AND THE BOMB

Seven years after dropping the atomic bombs that devastated the Japanese cities of Hiroshima and Nagasaki and brought World War II to an end, the United States exploded the world's first hydrogen bomb, a weapon hundreds of times more powerful than its predecessors. The blast, which took place in the remote Marshall Islands in the middle of the Pacific, obliterated a mile-wide atoll, leaving in its place a crater one-half mile deep and two miles across. From a searing pillar of fire, five times hotter than the sun, a lethal radioactive cloud billowed like a gargantuan cauliflower.

The development of the superbomb stemmed directly from the Cold War jockeying that followed World War II. After the Red Army occupied most of Eastern Europe, America's wartime alliance with Soviet dictator Joseph Stalin quickly collapsed, and the nation committed itself to containing Communist expansion worldwide. In the early years of the Cold War, America's exclusive possession of atomic weaponry gave it an immeasurable military and political advantage. But in August 1949 the Soviets smashed that monopoly with their own A-bomb. "There is only one thing worse than one nation having the atomic bomb," said Nobel Prize-winning chemist Harold C. Urey. "That's two nations having it." Now the dread of nuclear war joined the fear of Communism in casting a shadow over the good life promised by a booming postwar economy. Two

The radioactive cloud from the explosion of the world's first hydrogen bomb mushrooms to a height of 25 miles in the mid-Pacific sky on November 1, 1952. Scientists and military personnel witnessed the blast from ships and planes 50 miles away.

> "We have arrived at the point . . . where there is just no real alternative to peace."

Dwight D. Eisenhower

Red Army troops march in a 1954 Moscow parade celebrating the Bolshevik October Revolution of 1917 (above). Such warlike images emphasized the Soviet Union's overwhelming superiority in ground forces and exacerbated America's Cold War anxieties.

months after the Soviets' successful A-bomb test, the West grew still more jittery when Communist party chairman Mao Tse-tung established the People's Republic of China in October 1949, completing the takeover of the world's most populous nation from the regime of longtime U.S. ally Chiang Kai-shek.

Against this backdrop, President Harry Truman made his decision to pursue a superbomb—over the moral, political, and technical objections of an opposition whose principal spokesman was J. Robert Oppenheimer, the brilliant physicist who had led the development of the A-bomb *(pages 42-43)*. One of the most dogged promoters in the other camp was physicist Edward Teller, a staunch anti-Communist who had worked on the A-bomb project under Oppenheimer and who had since 1942 been exploring the idea of a bomb that would release energy by fusing atoms instead of splitting them, as did the A-bomb.

But to President Truman the decision turned on Moscow's capabilities. In January 1950 he met with Secretary of State Dean

Acheson, Secretary of Defense Louis Johnson, and Atomic Energy Commission chief David Lilienthal and asked them a critical question: Could the Russians build such a weapon? In answer, they all nodded yes. "In that case," Truman said, "we have no choice. We'll go ahead."

American military thinking was typified by Deputy Secretary of Defense Robert Lovett: "We must realize that we are now in a mortal conflict," he wrote in a secret memo calling for more defense spending. "It is not a cold war; it is a hot war." Lovett's position was apparently vindicated six months later when the Soviet-backed army of North Korea invaded South Korea in June 1950, prompting American intervention *(pages 82-85)*. As the nation attempted to stem the tide of Communism abroad, the crusade to crush it at home was intensifying. Senator Joseph R. McCarthy of Wisconsin *(pages 80-81),* whose name came to stand for the practice of hurling accusations of disloyalty without proof, became the leading crusader, but he was by no means alone. J. Edgar Hoover, director of the Federal Bureau of Investigation, had been ferreting out domestic Communists since the Red scare that followed World War I. Executive orders by President Truman and President Eisenhower called for wholesale loyalty reviews within the federal government. Hundreds of federal employees were dismissed on grounds of questionable loyalty, though none was proved to be a spy or saboteur.

A young congressman from California was catapulted into the Senate and then the Republican vice presidency by his forceful role in the House Un-American Activities Committee, called HUAC for short. "Traitors in the high councils in our own government," charged Richard M. Nixon, "have made sure that the deck is stacked on the Soviet side." As a result of HUAC hearings on the entertainment industry, scores of writers, composers, and performers accused of being Communists—or of simply being too liberal—were blacklisted by Hollywood, Broadway, radio, and television *(right)*.

HUAC's—and Nixon's—most compelling drama was the Pumpkin Papers Case, which pitted Whittaker Chambers, a self-confessed former Communist spy and a *Time* magazine editor,

Big Names on a Blacklist

Nearly 200 actors, singers, writers, composers, and others in the arts found it hard to get work after groups such as the House Un-American Activities Committee accused them of having Communist or left-wing political ties. Listed below are some of the most famous people who were blacklisted.

Leonard Bernstein Composer/Conductor

Lee J. Cobb Actor

Aaron Copland Composer

John Henry Faulk Radio Humorist

José Ferrer Actor

Will Geer Actor

Dashiell Hammet Writer

Lillian Hellman Playwright

Lena Horne Singer/Actress

Langston Hughes Poet

Ring Lardner Jr. Writer

Gypsy Rose Lee Striptease Artist

Albert Maltz Screenwriter

Arthur Miller Playwright

Louis Pollack Screenwriter

Paul Robeson Singer/Actor

Edward G. Robinson Actor

Pete Seeger Folk Singer

Dalton Trumbo Screenwriter

Orson Welles Actor/Director

Separated by a wire screen, Julius and Ethel Rosenberg leave federal court in a prison van after being convicted of espionage.

against Alger Hiss, a former State Department official. According to Chambers, Hiss had in the 1930s given him government documents that Chambers microfilmed, hid in a hollowed-out pumpkin on his Maryland farm, and eventually turned over to HUAC. Hiss denied the charges under oath but was convicted of perjury in 1950 and sent to prison.

America's search for subversives was fueled by a belief that the Soviets could not have built an atom bomb on their own, and six days after the Hiss conviction an arrest in England seemed to confirm that notion: Klaus Fuchs, a German-born English physicist, confessed to having passed atomic secrets to the Soviet Union while he worked on the A-bomb at Los Alamos, New Mexico, during the war. His testimony implicated others, notably Julius Rosenberg, a New York City electrical engineer, and his wife, Ethel *(page 78)*. A jury convicted the Rosenbergs of espionage, and federal judge Irving R. Kaufman sentenced them both to the electric chair.

The verdict set off an international furor. Many Americans agreed with Judge Kaufman's stern condemnation of the Rosenbergs: "Plain, deliberate, contemplated murder is dwarfed in magnitude by comparison with the crime you have committed." Others at home and in Europe insisted that guilty or not, the couple were victims of Cold War hysteria. On June 19, 1953, Julius and Ethel Rosenberg, who left two young sons, became the first native-born Americans to be put to death for espionage by order of a civilian court.

That same summer the United States once again lost nuclear dominance when the Soviets proved President Truman's advisers right by exploding a hydrogen bomb. To many, nuclear Armageddon seemed at hand. Renewed fear prompted increased civil defense and a mania for backyard bomb shelters *(pages 88-89)*. Then, in 1957, came a shock from out of the blue: Soviet scientists, rocketing ahead in missile technology, launched the earth's first artificial satellite, raising the specter of nuclear attack from space *(page 92)*. American anxiety reached a new high as the country found itself in the unhappy position of scrambling to catch up in the spiraling arms race.

> "Plain, deliberate . . . murder is dwarfed . . . by comparison with the crime you have committed."
>
> Federal judge Irving R. Kaufman, 1951

Reacting to widespread pleas for clemency after the Rosenbergs were sentenced to death, the demonstrators above picket the White House in favor of execution.

A Televised Showdown

During televised Senate hearings in 1954, U.S. Army special counsel Joseph Welch listens in disgust as Senator Joseph McCarthy attacks a young lawyer in Welch's firm. Welch's passionate response to the attack, excerpted below, helped bring the senator down.

McCarthy: *I think we should tell Mr. Welch that he has in his law firm a young man named Fisher who has been for a number of years a member of an organization named as the legal bulwark of the Communist Party. . . . Mr. Welch, I just felt that I had a duty to respond to your urgent request that before sundown, when we know of anyone serving the Communist cause, we let the agency know. . . . I have been rather bored with your phony requests to Mr. Cohn here that he personally get every Communist out of government before sundown.*

Welch: *Until this moment, Senator, I think I never really gauged your cruelty or your recklessness. Fred Fisher is starting what looks to be a brilliant career with us. Little did I dream you could be so reckless and so cruel as to do an injury to that lad. I fear he shall always bear a scar needlessly inflicted by you. . . . Let us not assassinate this lad further, Senator. You have done enough. Have you no sense of decency, sir, at long last? Have you left no sense of decency?*

The Rise and Fall of Tail-Gunner Joe

He bragged that he drank a fifth of whiskey a day. He lied about his service as a U.S. Marine officer during the war, dubbing himself Tail-Gunner Joe and claiming—falsely—that he had flown 30 combat missions in the Pacific. But few Americans had paid much attention to the swaggering, dark-jowled junior senator from Wisconsin until he made news with a sensational speech before a women's Republican club in Wheeling, West Virginia, on February 9, 1950. "I have here in my hand," he declared, waving a sheaf of papers, "a list of 205 names known to the secretary of state as being members of the Communist Party and who nevertheless are still working and shaping the policy of the State Department."

Joe McCarthy had found his calling. Carrying Cold War hysteria to new heights of innuendo and invective, he rode roughshod over the political landscape for the next four years. Democrats, he declared, were guilty of "20 years of treason," and George C. Marshall, a widely respected general in World War II and later secretary of state, was "an instrument of the Soviet conspiracy." He did not bother to back up accusations with evidence, and he raised character assassination to a high art. When a Senate subcommittee called the charges he had made in Wheeling "a fraud and a hoax," he retaliated against the chairman, Millard Tydings of Maryland. Circulating a faked photograph that purported to show Tydings chatting with a top American Communist, he helped torpedo Tydings's bid for reelection.

Despite his vicious tactics, McCarthy enjoyed the backing of Republican colleagues who wanted to discredit Democrats they considered "soft on Communism," and more than 50 percent of Americans polled said they supported him. President Eisenhower privately deplored McCarthyism but refused to "get into the gutter with that guy." After savaging the Democrats, McCarthy took on the U.S. Army. He tore into the brass for promoting a dentist who had once belonged to the Communist Party. The senator was in turn

McCarthy referred to his special counsel Roy Cohn, shown above with the senator at the army hearings, as "the most brilliant young fellow I have ever met." The cartoon at right by Herblock, a bitter critic who coined the word "McCarthyism," portrays the senator entangled in his own web of deceit.

accused of trying to get preferential treatment for David Schine, an aide who had been inducted into the army. McCarthy met his match in a dramatic televised encounter in May 1954 with U.S. Army special counsel Joseph Welch *(opposite)*. Millions of Americans saw McCarthy in action for the first time and recognized him as a cynical, bullying demagogue. In December a belatedly courageous Senate at last took action and condemned him. His liver ravaged by alcohol, Joe McCarthy died in 1957 at the age of 48.

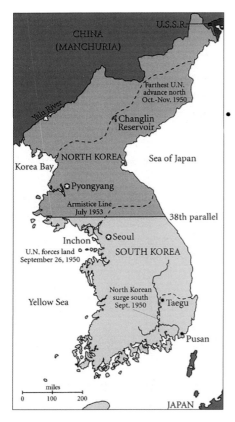

At the end of World War II, Korea was divided along the 38th parallel.

Korea's Human Cost

American Forces
Deaths: 33,629
Wounded and Missing: 103,284

Other U.N. Forces
Deaths: 2,550
Wounded and Missing: 9,076

**South Koreans
(military and civilian)**
Deaths: 591,285
Wounded and Missing: 1,293,592

**Communist Forces
(North Korea and China)**
Deaths: est. 1,347,000

A "Police Action" That Nobody Won

The Korean peninsula was a flash point left over from World War II. A Japanese colony since 1910, it had been divided after the war into two nations separated by the 38th parallel: Soviet-backed North Korea and U.S.-supported South Korea. On June 25, 1950, nearly 100,000 North Koreans smashed across the border and overran Seoul, the South Korean capital.

President Truman saw the invasion as a Soviet test of American resolve. "There's no telling what they'll do if we don't put up a fight right now," he said. Because the Soviets were boycotting the United

"There's no telling what they'll do if we don't put up a fight right now."

President Harry Truman, 1950

Nations Security Council at the time and were consequently not there to cast a veto, the U.N. approved sending a multinational force to defend South Korea. U.S. and South Korean troops made up about 90 percent of the force at its peak; its commander was General Douglas MacArthur, the fabled American hero of World War II.

At first only overwhelming air superiority prevented the U.N. forces from being driven into the sea. But in September MacArthur mounted a marine assault behind enemy lines at Inchon, 30 miles west of Seoul, in a bold stroke that cut off thousands of the enemy.

The numb, exhausted face of the marine (right) reflects the suffering that U.N. forces endured as they retreated from Chinese troops who launched a ferocious surprise attack across the Yalu River in late 1950.

Other U.N. troops pushed northward, reaching the 38th parallel by October 1.

MacArthur slashed on toward the Yalu River, the border with Communist China. Suddenly, a vanguard of more than one million Chinese assault troops swarmed across the Yalu, stunning U.N. forces. In some of the bloodiest combat ever endured by Americans, the Chinese drove them back into South Korea. By early 1951 U.N. resistance stiffened, and the opposing fronts stabilized near the 38th parallel.

MacArthur was burning to hammer China and North Korea into submission—with atomic weapons if necessary. The president, however, feared an all-out attack could ignite a third world war. Determined to negotiate an end to the conflict, he ordered the general to keep his opinions to himself. But in April 1951 MacArthur arrogantly disobeyed orders and went public with his strategy, declaring, "There is no substitute for victory!" Truman promptly fired him, in a move that outraged millions of Americans.

After two more years of fighting, North Korea agreed to a cease-fire in July 1953. The truce left the two Koreas still divided and virtually devastated.

Weary marines follow a vehicle filled with corpses as U.S. forces retreat from North Korea. Trapped near the Chosin Reservoir, the troops had to fight their way to Hamhung, some 40 miles away, for evacuation.

Duck and Cover!

I cannot tell you when or where the attack will come or that it will come at all," President Truman told the nation in 1950. "I can only remind you that we must be ready when it does come." With those chilling words, he launched the Civil Defense Administration—and a challenge that frightened, bewildered, and sometimes amused Americans. They were to think the unthinkable: that they could somehow survive the blast, heat, and radiation of a direct nuclear attack.

Schools added a new subject known as duck and cover. On command, students were taught to crouch, shield their eyes, and seek cover under any available shelter, including their desks. Parents were assured that children would be safe in school and could be picked up when the all clear sounded. Just in case, however, some schools issued military-style dog tags to identify students after an attack.

Civil defense manuals issued by the federal government, with titles such as *The Family Fallout Shelter* and *Education for National Survival,* urged homeowners to install shatterproof windows and buy Geiger counters to measure ambient radiation. "Your chances of living through an atomic attack are much better than you thought," reassured one manual. "At Nagasaki, almost 70 percent of the people a mile from the bomb lived to tell their experience." To improve their chances, 1 in every 20 Americans either modified their homes to include basement-based shelters with reinforced framing or acquired the ultimate in family protection by arranging for an underground bomb shelter in their backyards *(pages 88-89).*

With crayons and paper neatly aligned atop their desks, schoolchildren demonstrate the approved duck and cover routine during an air-raid drill in St. Petersburg, Florida. Signs to the nearest fallout shelter (above) became a familiar sight all over the United States.

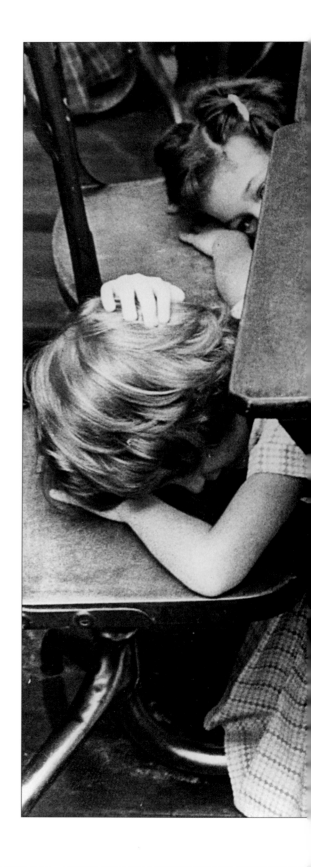

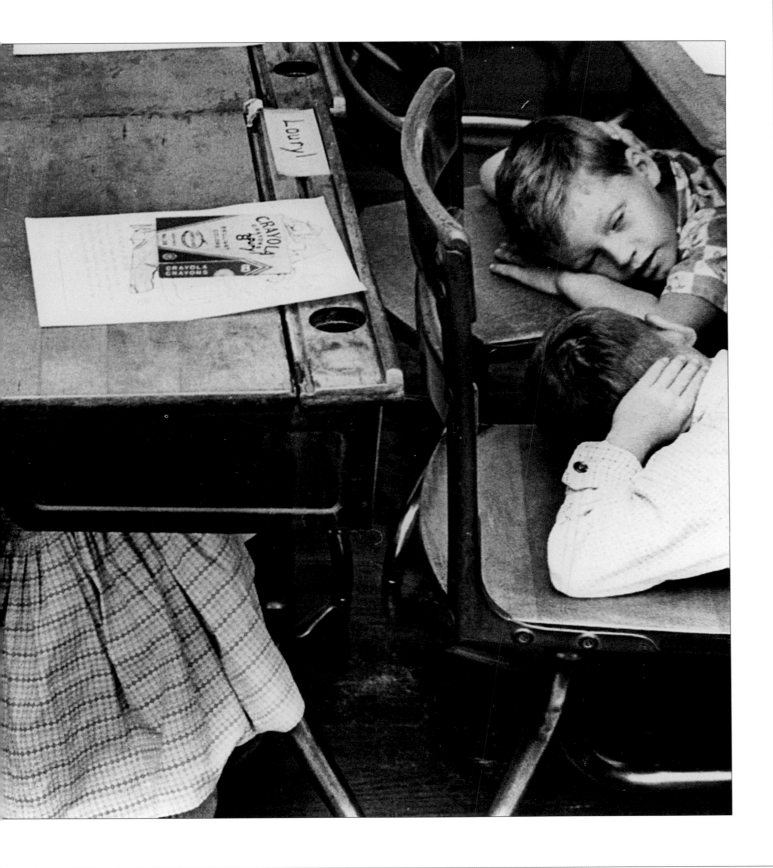

A Hideaway for Five

One of several measures encouraged by the civil-defense authorities, the fallout shelter at right was supposed to keep a family of five safe and snug even if a hydrogen bomb exploded only three miles away. Manufactured by the Walter Kidde Nuclear Laboratories in response to government urging, the Kidde Kokoon was a steel tank measuring eight feet by 14 feet and was designed to be buried three feet deep. The $3,000 luxury model came equipped for a five-day stay, with canned food and water, a radio, and a generator. The shelter also included protective suits that could be worn above ground after the attack. Families could also pack books, games, and hobby supplies to while away the time underground.

A survivor could measure radiation with the hand-held Geiger counter with earphones at right. About the size of a shoebox, it indicated radiation intensity with clicks—the faster the clicks, the more dangerous the conditions.

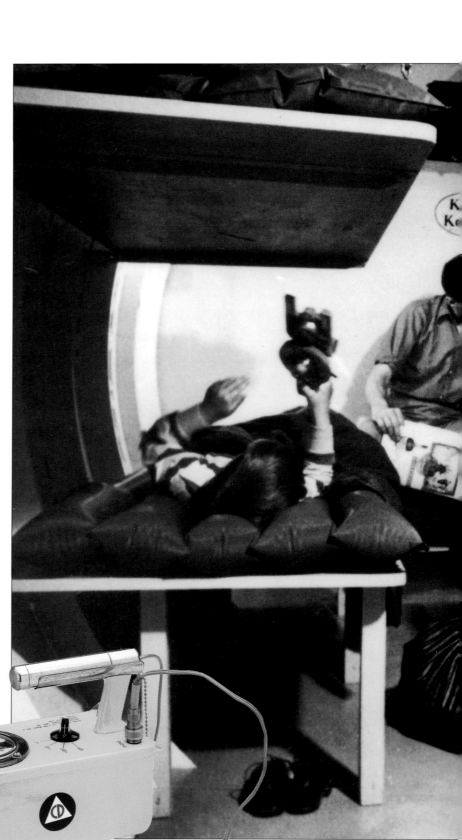

Doomsday Hits Home

To create a sense of urgency in Americans and to promote bomb shelters, civil defense officials pointed to such awesome demonstrations of the power of the A-bomb as the one shown here. It was just one of scores of nuclear tests conducted in the Nevada desert to evaluate nuclear devices and their impact.

But the tests backfired in some quarters of the public. An outcry arose when scientists discovered that radioactive strontium 90 from drifting fallout was being deposited in the bones of babies living far from any test site. Movements sprang up calling for a ban on testing and for nuclear disarmament, and partly as a result both the United States and the Soviet Union halted aboveground testing in 1958.

When the testing stopped, few American families had their own bomb shelter. The majority had been deterred by both the expense and the conviction that a shelter would be useless in an attack. One Los Angeles woman who had invested $1,995 in a backyard shelter decided it could serve as a root cellar and a playhouse for her three children.

The sequence of photos at right shows the effects of a small atomic test in 1953 on a house two-thirds of a mile from ground zero. Brilliantly illuminated in the first millisecond (top), the house is then scorched, engulfed in flame, shattered by the shock wave, and—in less than two seconds—ripped to pieces.

A mother and child protest nuclear war during a boycott of an air-raid drill in New York City.

THERE IS NO SHELTER IN NUCLEAR WAR

I WANT TO GROW UP

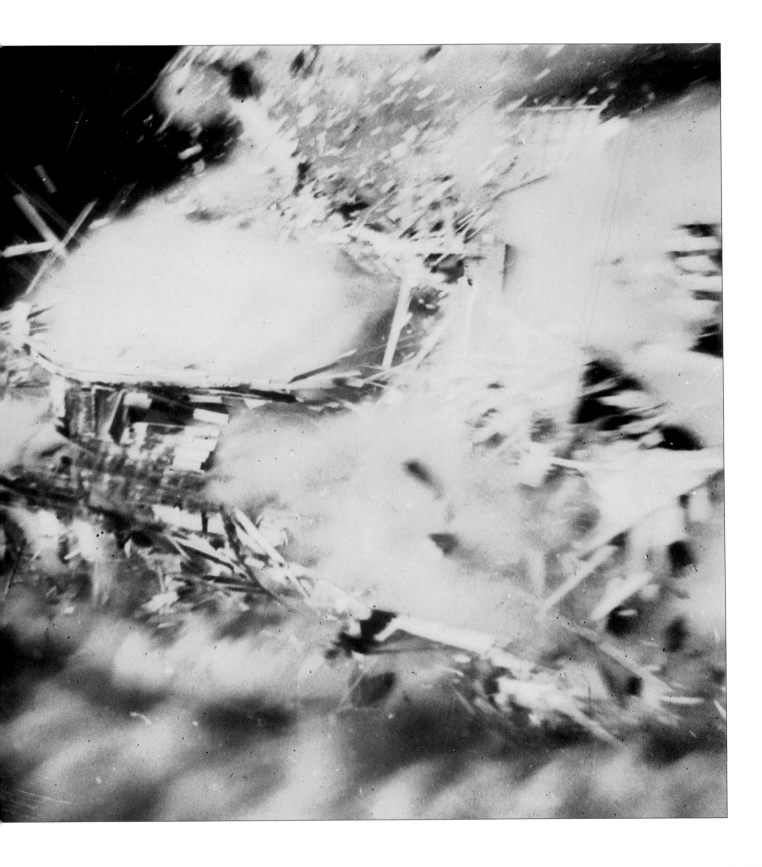

The Specter of Sputnik

In the fall of 1957, Americans anxiously scanned the sky just before dawn or after sunset for the tiny sunlit speck that ushered in the space age on October 4. Launched by the Soviet Union, Sputnik (Russian for fellow traveler) was the world's first artificial satellite—a 184-pound, beachball-sized sphere stuffed with eerily beeping radio transmitters. A month later it was joined by Sputnik II, a half-ton companion that carried a dog named Laika.

Americans reacted with shock and disbelief. The Soviets' sensational Sputniks dealt a serious blow to the prestige of U.S. science and technology, and they also raised the specter of attack by powerful rockets carrying nuclear warheads or from killer satellites in outer space. Meanwhile, Soviet Premier Nikita Khrushchev gloated about his nation's triumph. A year earlier he had boasted, "History is on our side. We will bury you." Now he bragged about the rockets that boosted the Sputniks into orbit and predicted his comrades would soon be "turning out long-range missiles like sausages."

Public alarm mounted in Decem-

Above, a model of Sputnik I shows how radio antennas extended from the satellite's spherical body.

In typical form during a tour of the United States in 1959, Soviet Premier Nikita Khrushchev drives home his point at a press conference in Washington, D.C.

"We will bury you."

Nikita Khrushchev

ber when the intended U.S. reply, a Vanguard rocket carrying a grapefruit-sized satellite, rose two feet off the launch pad at Cape Canaveral and blew up. The failure earned such names as "Stay-putnik" and "Flopnik."

Americans breathed easier when a Jupiter C rocket finally got an Explorer satellite aloft nearly four months after *Sputnik I*. The nation was now a credible competitor in the new cold-war arena. And it was soon to expand: President Eisenhower established the National Aeronautics and Space Administration, which selected the first seven astronauts and began developing a craft for them to fly. The race to explore space firsthand, as well as by proxy, was on.

Specially designed to celebrate Buick's 50th anniversary in 1953, the limited-edition Skylark convertible sported a chopped-down windshield, rakish styling, and a V-8 engine.

America's Dream Machines

★

THE HEYDAY OF CAR CULTURE

When 26-year-old Charles Schulz landed the contract for his "Peanuts" comic strip in October 1950, it seemed to him there was just one way to mark the occasion. "I bought the first car that anyone in our family had ever owned," the cartoonist wrote, "and it was a beauty." Each night after parking the lime green Ford, he recalled, he "would always turn around to look back at my car, shining under the streetlights, and be so proud."

Automobiles in the 1950s were anything but basic transportation. A car was status, freedom, and personal identity. Many Americans had spent the Depression and the war years nursing along worn-out clunkers. Others, like Schulz, had never had a car at all. Now, rising incomes and easy credit brought late-model automobiles within reach, and by the end of the decade four out of five American households had a car.

Although some single people had their own transportation—including a few sporty foreign cars—the typical automobile of the 1950s was a family car. Parked prominently in the driveway, a gleaming automobile was the crowning touch to the suburban good life. Many families washed and polished their prized vehicle every weekend, then piled in for a satisfying Sunday drive.

Much as Americans loved their automobiles, however, they didn't hold on to any one vehicle for long. On average, car owners in the 1950s traded in old dream machines for new ones every two years.

Cars With Personality

Cars had so much character in the 1950s that most people could easily tell them apart. A long, flat Ford wasn't likely to be mistaken for a high-roofed Chrysler or a muscular General Motors car. Perhaps the most distinctive American automobiles were two rival sports cars: the Chevrolet Corvette and the Ford Thunderbird. The Thunderbird had a simple shape, almost no chrome, and huge taillights. The Corvette—typified by the model

How Much Did It Cost?

1951 Nash Rambler	$1,732
1957 Chevrolet Bel Air	$2,238
1953 Kaiser Manhattan	$2,650
1957 Ford Thunderbird	$3,408
1960 Chevrolet Corvette	$3,872
1956 Cadillac Series 62	$4,711

1951 Nash Rambler

1960 Chevrolet Corvette

1957 Chevrolet Bel Air

shown below that was introduced in late 1959—was designed with curving European lines that to American eyes looked like nothing on earth. Four decades later, a former gas station attendant vividly recalled his first sight of one as a teenager: "Suddenly this apparition pulled up to the pump—a white, low, sleek, racy-looking coupe of no recognizable lineage whatsoever, except that it said 'Chevrolet' on it. It was like a flying saucer had landed. It was a Corvette."

Can I Get It in Pink?

From Chiffon Green to Tango Red, car paint names were as fanciful as car styles in the 1950s. The colorful selections below are just some of those that Chrysler purchasers could choose from during the 1955 model year.

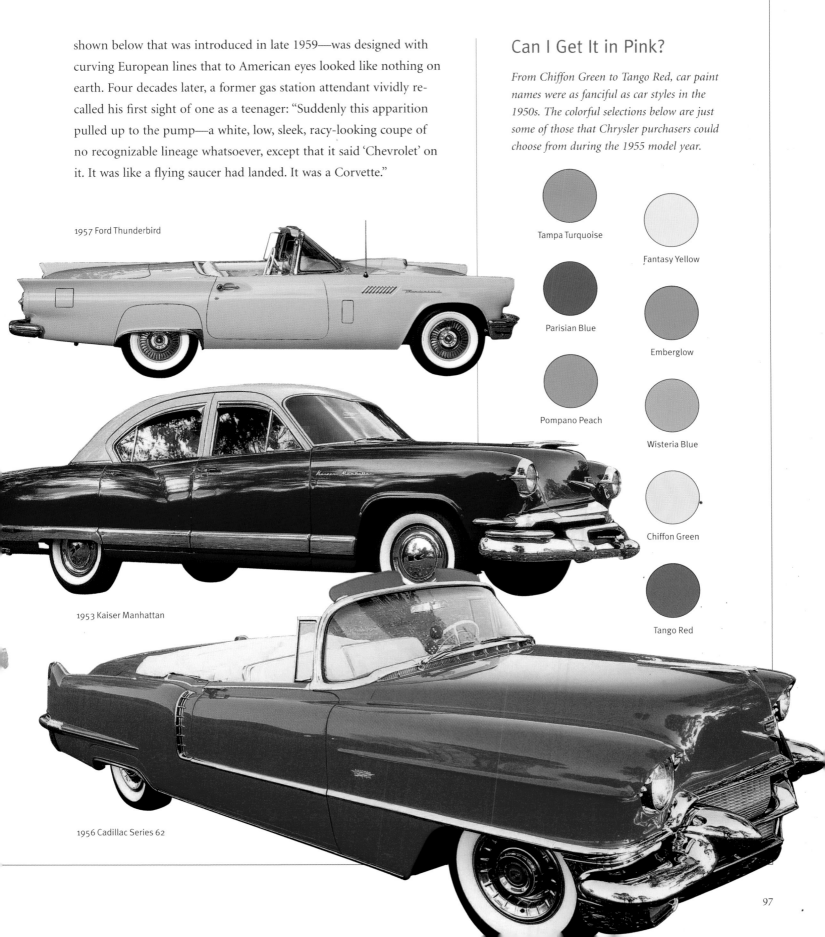

1957 Ford Thunderbird

Tampa Turquoise

Fantasy Yellow

Parisian Blue

Emberglow

Pompano Peach

Wisteria Blue

Chiffon Green

Tango Red

1953 Kaiser Manhattan

1956 Cadillac Series 62

1959 Chevrolet Impala   1960 Studebaker Lark

Gleaming Grilles and Flying Fins

Late in the 1940s, General Motors stylist Harley Earl added airplane-style details to GM's cars—first small fins reminiscent of a twin-tailed fighter plane, then grilles that looked like jet-engine intake ducts. Other manufacturers followed suit. Then came 1957, when Chrysler, touting its "flight-sweep," "Forward Look" styling, stretched fins to flamboyant new extremes. The fin frenzy that followed reached its apex in the 1959 Cadillacs, whose rear ends stood three and a half feet tall *(below, far right)*.

1958 Cadillac Series 62   1960 Plymouth Fury

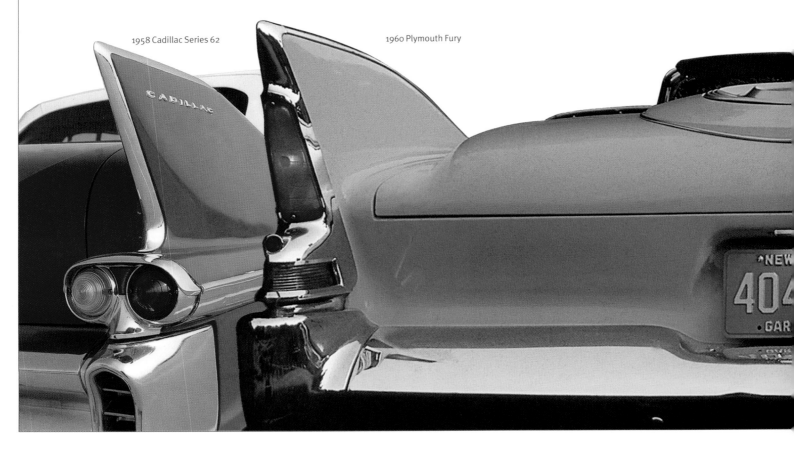

1954 Hudson Hornet

1958 Buick Roadmaster 75

Protruding taillights—no fewer than three on each fin of the 1958 DeSotos—pointed aft like afterburner flames.

Car design had become a business of style over substance—and the public loved it. By contrast, seat belts and safety features were unpopular extras. Safety was for "squares," one executive told *Fortune* magazine, adding, "and there ain't no squares anymore." At decade's end the exuberant styles lost popularity as fast as they had gained it. Fins all but vanished after the early 1960s.

Flashing chrome and soaring fins spelled automotive distinction in the mid to late '50s and right up to 1960-model-year cars like the Studebaker Lark shown opposite and the Plymouth Fury below, both introduced in late 1959.

1959 Cadillac Sedan de Ville

Born to Lose

Ford thought it had the car to beat for the 1958 model year. The price was right, the dealer network was in place, and the public relations buildup was among the most intense ever concocted. Nine years in the planning, the Edsel, named for founder Henry Ford's son, made its debut on September 4, 1957. It was a total loser.

The timing bore some of the blame. The country was beginning to slip into a recession that hurt car sales, and small vehicles like the Volkswagen were starting to attract interest. But the real problem was the Edsel itself: It was ugly, and its ugliest feature was its oval grille. People said it looked like a horse collar, a toilet seat, or a mouth that had just sucked a lemon. Ford tried a hasty restyling, but the Edsel was beyond saving. After racking up a loss estimated at $350 million, it was withdrawn from the market in 1959.

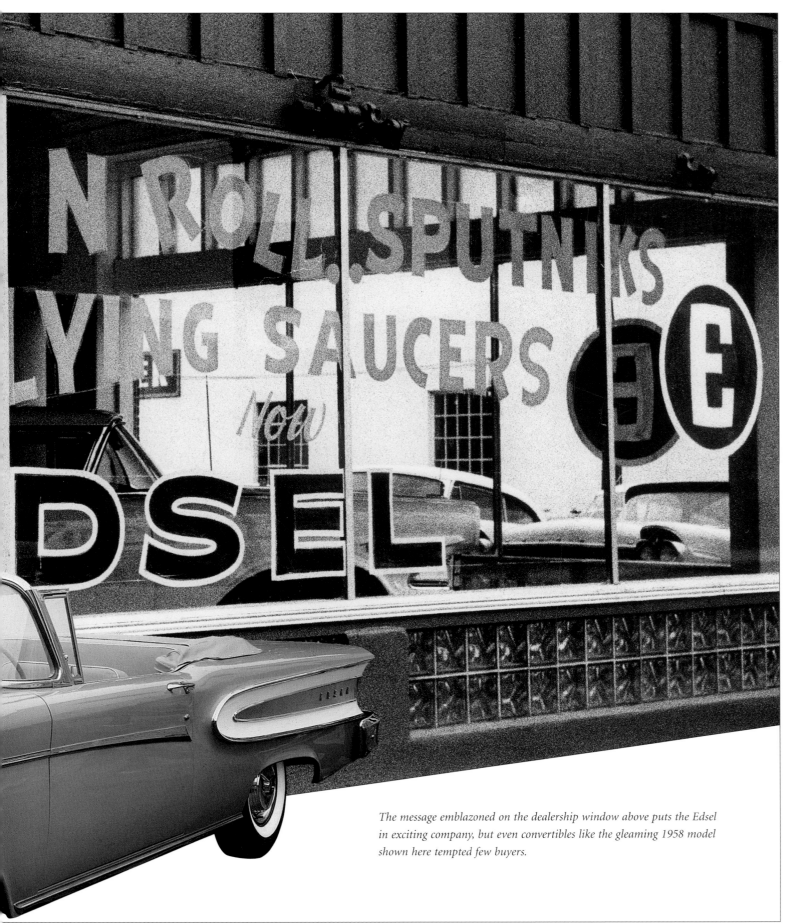

The message emblazoned on the dealership window above puts the Edsel in exciting company, but even convertibles like the gleaming 1958 model shown here tempted few buyers.

New Jersey Turnpike
pennant

"See the USA in your Chevrolet."

Chevrolet ad campaign

A price war rages between a Mobil station (foreground) and its competitor across the road. As fill-ups became big business, national chains replaced many independent stations.

Hitting the Road

s I was motorvatin' over the hill, I saw Maybellene in a Coupe DeVille," sang Chuck Berry in his 1955 hit "Maybellene." His listeners pictured the scene instantly, because they were spending their time on the highways, too. Americans drove several hundred billion miles every year of the decade, fueling a burst of roadside businesses that included McDonald's, Kentucky Fried Chicken, Howard Johnson's Motor Lodge, and Holiday Inn. In most regions of the country, road building lagged badly behind the increasing traffic. The solution came in 1956, when Congress authorized construction of the interstate highway system—perhaps the most enduring legacy of the automobile decade.

Road maps

Car decal

Mobilgas pump

Motel postcard

Advertisement for Coca-Cola

Magnolia Gas curb sign

Gas station logos

Roadside businesses lured drivers with bold signs, free maps, and advertisements like those shown here, while decals recorded vacation itineraries. License plates (above) had distinctive shapes and sizes in the '50s.

Car Mania

The beaming driver of the pint-sized Corvette above and the crew-cut crowd in the Volkswagen at far right were typical '50s Americans—positively car crazy. It seemed for a while as though anything was more fun if a car—the newer and bigger, the better—was involved. At a time when conventional movie theaters were closing by the hundreds, drive-in theaters flourished, increasing from a few hundred to more than 3,000 over the course of the decade. Auto-enthused entrepreneurs founded everything from drive-in restaurants, which sprang up all over the country, to novelties like drive-in banks and laundries. The ultimate car experience for most people was to go on vacation in the family car—a fact borne out by National Park Service statistics. By the end of the 1950s, almost 27 million tourists, most in their own vehicles, were visiting national parks every year—nearly twice as many as when the decade began.

Above, the pastor of a Florida drive-in church preaches to his parked congregation in 1955. Below, a carhop serves teenagers at a drive-in diner.

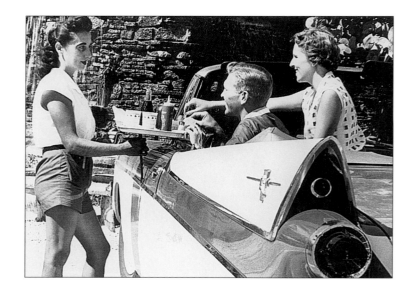

Forty college students cram into a Volkswagen in a 1956 stunt.

Charlton Heston as Moses in The Ten Commandments plays to a full house at a Utah drive-in theater in 1958. By the late 1950s, there were huge drive-ins accommodating as many as 2,000 vehicles; most had room for several hundred.

The Fight for Equal Rights

★

A NEW ASSAULT ON OLD JIM CROW

She was 15, neatly dressed and determined to attend the first day of school. That intention, sanctioned by recent Supreme Court decisions, was sufficient to attract a mob of rowdy whites who shouted curses and worse. "Lynch her!" someone yelled. "Lynch her!" In 1957, in Little Rock, Arkansas, the dark underside of the American Dream was unfolding, and it was a national nightmare.

Nearly a century after the abolition of slavery, racial discrimination persisted in all of the United States but most blatantly in the South. There, bias was embodied in a rigid system of segregation dictated by state and local laws. Black southerners attended segregated schools, rode in separate sections of public transportation, and even drank at water fountains marked "for colored only." These laws were widely known by the name Jim Crow—a term that had originated in 19th-century minstrel shows making fun of blacks. Under an 1896 Supreme Court decision, Jim Crow laws were also constitutional; seven out of eight justices ruled that year that segregation was legal so long as equal accommodations were provided for blacks.

During the 1950s, blacks and other civil rights activists mounted successful legal assaults on that longstanding decision. But as the bastions of segregation slowly began to crumble, southern whites unleashed a powerful backlash of hate.

Wearing a new dress she made for her first day at Little Rock Central High School, Elizabeth Eckford braves jeering whites. Moments later she was turned away by National Guardsmen on the governor's orders.

A Landmark Legal Victory

SEGREGATION IN PUBLIC SCHOOLS OUTLAWED BY U. S. SUPREME COURT

Atlanta Daily World

CITY EDITION

FHA To Honor Farm Families Today At Fort Valley State

Chief Justice Warren Reads Court's Unanimous Decision

Significance Of Decision Aired By City Leaders

REVIEWING THE NEWS

For The Negro There Will Be No Violence

Five attacks on school segrega-tion reached the Supreme Court in 1952, with cases origi-nating in South Carolina, Delaware, Virginia, Kansas, and the District of Columbia. The justices consolidated all five under one name: *Brown v. the Board of Education of Topeka, Kansas.* Oliver Brown, a welder, had sued on behalf of his daughter Linda, shown at left in 1953. In order to attend a run-down black school, Linda walked six blocks through a dangerous railroad switching yard, then took a bus another 21 blocks; a better white school stood only seven blocks from her home. In the photograph at right, she crosses the yard with her six-year-old sister Terry Lynn. The lead counsel for the NAACP's Legal Defense Fund

was Thurgood Marshall. A tall, folksy advocate who had won 13 of 15 previous cases before the High Court, Marshall argued that segregated schooling deprived black children of the equal protection guaranteed by the 14th Amendment. Key to his case was evidence from psychologists that segregation damaged black youngsters, making them feel inferior.

Months passed, yet the Court hesitated to make a ruling. In the meantime Chief Justice Fred Vinson, who likely would have supported segregation, died. He was succeeded by Earl Warren, a former Republican governor of California, who led his colleagues toward a unanimous decision announced on May 17, 1954. "In the field of public education the doctrine of 'separate but equal' has no place. Separate educational facilities are inherently unequal."

Reaction to the landmark ruling was swift. Segregationists rushed to condemn the decision—and defy it. State legislatures prepared laws to abolish public schools rather than see them integrated. Middle-class whites, wearing suits instead of Ku Klux Klan sheets, joined White Citizens' Councils to block desegregation through economic intimidation and even violence. But the victory also heartened black citizens long used to segregation, inspiring new protests like the Montgomery bus boycott *(pages 114-117)*.

Rioting against school integration in Clinton, Tennessee, in 1956—two years after the Brown decision—a white mob rocks an out-of-state car whose black occupants were just passing through town.

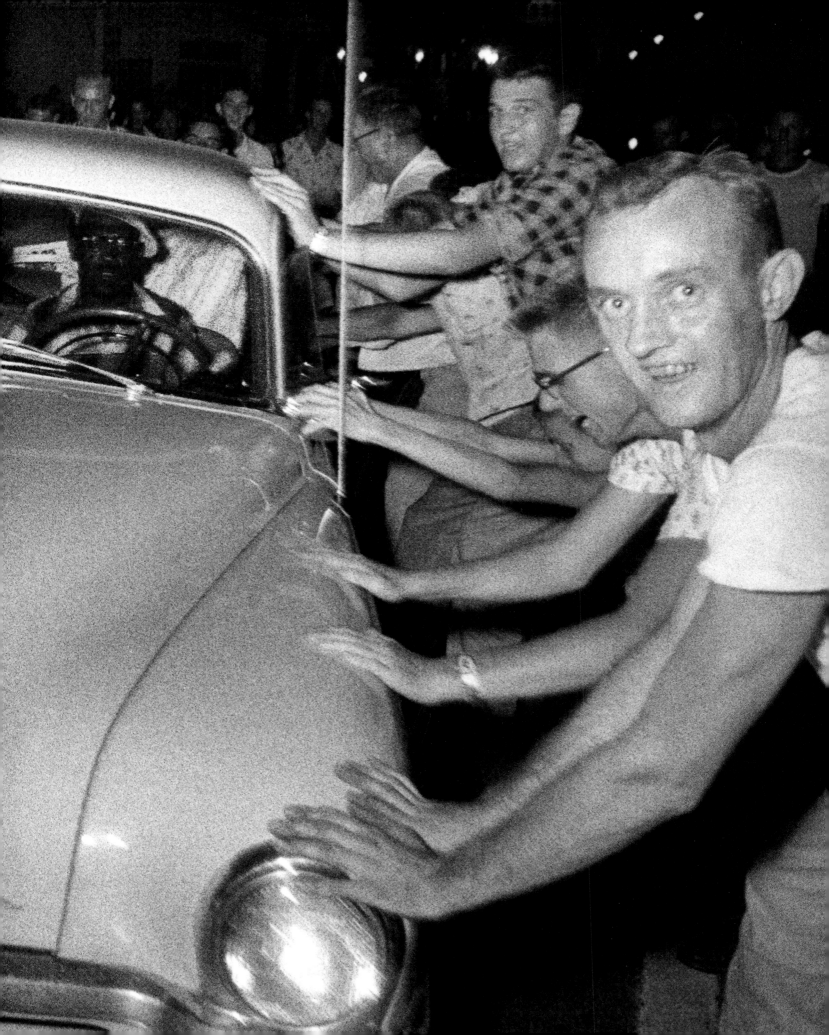

The Boycott That Began a Movement

R osa Parks had endured the indignities of the bus service in Montgomery, Alabama, for most of her 42 years. It was not just that blacks had to sit in the back of the bus. If the white section filled up, black passengers had to stand. On Friday evening, December 1, 1955, Parks had worked all day as a tailor's assistant at a downtown department store, then shopped for groceries. When the driver ordered her to give up her seat to a white man, she refused and was arrested.

Parks, who radiated a gentle dignity, was a churchwoman and former official in the local NAACP. Her arrest gave the city's black leaders, who had long resented the bus policy, an ideal case to rally around. That Monday, blacks in Montgomery boycotted the buses. Thousands attending a mass meeting then voted to keep the protest going. They also formed a committee, electing as its leader the 26-year-old pastor of Dexter Avenue Baptist Church, Martin Luther King Jr. The young minister quickly showed an ability to speak to his listeners' hearts. "We are tired," he declared, "tired of being segregated and humiliated; tired of being kicked about by the brutal feet of oppression."

The boycotters' original demands were modest. They were not asking for desegregation of the buses, but merely courtesy from drivers, segregated seating filled on a first-come, first-served basis, and the hiring of some black drivers. Instead, city commissioners tried to thwart the protest at every turn. When black-owned cabs hauled customers for 10 cents a ride—the same as bus fare—the city threatened to shut them down for charging less than the lawful minimum.

The black community responded with a carpool that mustered more than 300 volunteer drivers. Some white housewives even co-

Rosa Parks, whose refusal to give up her seat to a white man ignited the boycott, is fingerprinted in February 1956 after her arrest under an antiboycott law.

During the boycott, a lone white rider occupies a bus. Blacks had accounted for more than 75 percent of passengers. Below, women wait at a carpool dispatch station. Others simply walked. "My feets is weary," said one elderly woman, "but my soul is rested."

Protest leader Martin Luther King Jr. poses for a police mug shot after his arrest for conspiracy to boycott.

operated by chauffeuring their maids. When local agents began canceling liability insurance for the carpool, the boycotters reached across the Atlantic to Lloyd's of London for coverage.

Even after his own house was bombed, King preached nonviolence. Taking his philosophy from Christ and his tactics from the passive resistance of India's Mohandas Gandhi, he counseled his followers to "meet hate with love." As a practical matter, King's approach cast the reasonable, civil boycotters in an increasingly positive light as the city government became ever more hostile. When 89 of the protesters, including Parks and King, were arrested for breaking an old antiboycott law, the result was national, and largely favorable, publicity.

Meanwhile, the protesters went to court asking for an outright end to Jim Crow buses. On November 13, 1956, the Supreme Court agreed, affirming a lower court's ruling that laws requiring bus segregation were unconstitutional. After 381 days, the boycott ended in victory. Its effects reached far beyond one city's transit system, inspiring a movement aimed at attaining equal rights through nonviolent protest.

Free on bond after conviction for conspiracy to boycott, King gets a kiss from his wife, Coretta, and cheers from supporters. The guilty verdict was cause for celebration because it brought world attention to the boycott.

Explosive Battle to Go to School

Although the Supreme Court had decreed that school desegregation proceed "with all deliberate speed," the pace frequently was agonizingly slow. By the fall of 1957, three years after the *Brown* decision, seven southern states had enrolled not a single black child in white schools and had no plans to do so. Progress in 10 other previously segregated states and the District of Columbia ranged from real desegregation to black enrollment so sparse that it constituted only token integration.

During that autumn in Nashville, Tennessee, even token efforts were too much for many white folks. The school board, under a federal court order, had diligently prepared for the enrollment of 13 handpicked black first graders in five previously white elementary schools. Nonetheless, black parents escorting these children to school on the first day had to guide them through a gauntlet of hostile whites bearing Confederate flags and angry signs. That night the enmity escalated. A thunderous blast of dynamite shattered a wing of the Hattie Cotton Elementary School, which had enrolled a single black five-year-old girl.

To Nashville's credit, city authorities refused to be intimidated. When white segregationists rallied outside schools the following morning, they faced barricades and armed policemen who ensured the safe arrival of black children and their parents. This official conduct contrasted dramatically with Tennessee's neighbor, Arkansas *(pages 120-121)*. There, the governor of the state, instead of invoking his authority to uphold the law, was employing it illegally in an attempt to maintain the lily white makeup of the schools in Little Rock.

Black first graders and their parents get a police escort to one of Nashville's five newly integrated elementary schools. Police also confiscated weapons and cracked down on white troublemakers.

Detectives and reporters inspect the damage at Nashville's Hattie Cotton School after a dynamite blast climaxed integration protests. The mother of the only black child enrolled there later transferred her to a black school.

While a policeman stands guard in the background, Hattie Cotton's principal, Margaret Cate, examines a mangled book in the bomb-torn ruins of the library.

Battle Lines at Central High

N o one expected the biggest crisis in school integration to erupt in Little Rock, Arkansas. Soon after the *Brown* decision, the school board had approved a plan for gradual desegregation starting at the high-school level. Arkansas's law and medical schools already had been integrated nearly a decade before. Governor Orval Faubus, though scarcely a liberal, was not ranked among the South's fire-breathing racists.

But Faubus had an acute feel for the sentiments of poor white people like his own forebears, and he badly wanted another term as governor. In September 1957, shrewdly sensing the rising hostility toward racial change, Faubus called out the Arkansas National Guard. His pretext was to prevent violence at Little Rock Central High School, but his true purpose was to thwart the scheduled enrollment of nine black students. Guardsmen allowed whites to harass the students and then, on the governor's orders, barred their entry. Two weeks later, Faubus grudgingly complied with a federal judge's order to remove the guard but did nothing to discourage the daily mob. When city police managed to slip the black students into school a few days later, the crowd outside beat up newsmen and became so unruly that the students had to be removed. President Eisenhower, whose conservatism balked at forced integration, hesitated to act. But the nation's revulsion at daily newspaper and TV images depicting outright defiance of federal law forced his hand. He federalized the Arkansas National Guard and sent in 1,000 soldiers from the famed 101st Airborne Division. The next day, paratroopers dispersed the mob and escorted the black students up the front steps of Central High. "For the first time in my life," said 15-year-old Minnijean Brown, "I feel like an American citizen."

With bayonets fixed on their rifles, U.S. troops escort black students into Little Rock Central High School on September 25, 1957.

Art and Entertainment

★

LEISURE COMES OF AGE

Along with houses and cars, living-room sets and refrigerators, middle-class Americans consumed culture—lowbrow, middlebrow, and highbrow—with gusto in the '50s. *Business Week* magazine noted, "Never have so many people had so much time on their hands—with pay." Some critics predicted that Americans would spend all of their newfound leisure hours watching television and become "squint-eyed, hunchbacked and fond of the dark."

In fact, there was an explosion of creativity in the worlds of art and entertainment. Television did keep many former moviegoers at home, but Hollywood stars kept the old magic alive despite a shrinking audience. Books like the bestseller *Kon-Tiki* *(inset)* poured off the presses in record numbers, a generation of young artists struck off in groundbreaking new directions, and a glittering series of brand-new Broadway musicals debuted, from *Guys and Dolls* in 1950 to *The Sound of Music* in 1959.

In popular music, Americans enjoyed a steady parade of new hits from such appealing vocalists as fresh-faced Rosemary Clooney and likeable Perry Como with his trademark sweater. But by mid-decade, change was in the air, as Americans got their first earful of the revolutionary music called rock and roll.

At right, Dean Martin and Jerry Lewis jump for joy in 1951, a year in which they were the top money-earning act in show business. The popular comedy team costarred in 17 movies between 1949 and 1956.

Movieland Endures

Hollywood's like Egypt," moaned producer David O. Selznick in 1951. "Full of crumbling pyramids. . . . It'll just keep on crumbling until finally the wind blows the last studio prop across the sands." Selznick's lament was not much of an exaggeration. Movies had once been the country's number one source of entertainment, but in 1950 Americans spent more on fishing gear and bowling than on movie tickets. Attendance had shrunk to 36 million people a week from a record high of 82 million in 1946.

The sharp decline had several causes, including the lasting impact of a 1948 Supreme Court decision that all but dismantled the old Hollywood studio system. But by far the biggest threat was television, which offered viewers entertainment in their own living rooms. Jack Warner of Warner Bros. tried to make light of the importance of TV, declaring that it was merely a passing phase. But he tacitly admitted how threatening the medium was when he decreed that no home shown in a Warner Bros. movie could contain a TV set.

Despite its financial woes, however, Hollywood produced a host of classic pictures in the '50s, with casts that included familiar faces like Judy Garland and Gary Cooper, both shown here, as well as new stars like Marilyn Monroe and Marlon Brando *(pages 128-131)*. Competition with TV also inspired moviemakers to pursue technological advances like improved color and wide-screen formats such as CinemaScope. Movies became more permissive, too, defying standards long enforced by the industry-sponsored Motion Picture Production Code. *The Moon Is Blue,* a frothy romantic comedy, raised a censorship rumpus in 1954 when the code denied the movie its seal of approval because the characters joked about adultery and used such words as "seduction" and "pregnant." Producer-director Otto Preminger distributed the movie anyway, and the public flocked to it in droves.

Judy Garland rests while filming A Star Is Born. Her brilliant performance in the 1954 drama was a triumph after difficult times that included divorce and attempted suicide.

Hollywood veteran Gary Cooper, a leading man since the 1920s, won an Oscar for his role as sheriff Will Kane (right) in the 1952 Western High Noon.

The Epic

Bigness was a weapon that moviemakers aimed at television's weak spot. As one canny studio head remarked, "How can anyone watch a big picture on that little box?" Unheard-of-millions were lavished on wide-screen, action-packed epics featuring platoons of big-name stars, extras by the thousands, and panoramic views of exotic locations.

The most colossal of the colossal epics was MGM's *Ben-Hur,* starring Charlton Heston in the title role of a Jewish patriot in Roman-ruled Palestine in the early days of Christianity. According to the studio's massive publicity campaign, the movie was filmed on more than 300 sets with 10,000 extras, 100,000 costumes, and a million props. A lake was constructed for the sea battles, which featured a life-sized Roman warship, and the 18-acre arena for the chariot race shown at right was modeled on Rome's Circus Maximus. At 15 million dollars, *Ben-Hur* was the costliest movie yet produced. And the investment paid off handsomely: *Ben-Hur* earned more than 80 million dollars and won 11 Academy Awards.

Charlton Heston (right) fends off the whip of his mortal enemy, Messala, in a chariot race that ran nine minutes on the screen and cost one million dollars to film.

Glittering Goddesses

More than anything else, it was the stars that kept Americans going to the movies in the '50s. Each of the four leading ladies pictured here possessed a unique combination of glamour, beauty, elegance, and sex appeal, and each had her own retinue of fans who followed the fortunes of their favorite movie queen both on screen and off.

None of the gorgeous blondes vying to be Hollywood's sex goddess of the '50s could hold a candle to Marilyn Monroe. She projected an enchanting contrariness on the screen—innocent one minute, naughty the next, and always desirable. Monroe achieved stardom in the 1953 comedy Gentlemen Prefer Blondes, which was quickly followed by another success, How to Marry a Millionaire. Her fans were now legion, and when The Seven Year Itch was being shot in New York in 1955, thousands of them materialized on a street corner at 2:00 a.m. to gawk and cheer as her skirt caught a revealing updraft from a subway vent (right).

The epitome of cool blonde beauty, Grace Kelly dazzled audiences with what Alfred Hitchcock called her "sexual elegance." He directed her in the 1954 thriller Rear Window with James Stewart, in which she played a well-bred Park Avenue fashion editor whose polished exterior concealed a smoldering sensuality (above). That same year, Kelly won a Best Actress Oscar for her portrayal of the dowdy, bespectacled wife of alcoholic singer Bing Crosby in The Country Girl, a role that cast her against type and showed her breadth as an actress. She traded her career as a celluloid princess for a role as the real thing when she married Prince Rainier III of Monaco in 1956 (pages 50-51).

Brigitte Bardot

And God Created Woman _opened with a shot that gave many Americans their first taste of French insouciance about nudity: Brigitte Bardot (left) lay "stretched end to end of the CinemaScope screen, bottoms up and bare as a censor's eyeball,"_ Time _magazine reported. The unabashed eroticism of the "sex kitten" drew both enthusiastic audiences and denunciations. The movie was banned in numerous cities and labeled "dirt for dirt's sake" and "an assault on each and every woman of our . . . nation, living and dead." Still, Bardot became a favorite foreign actress of the '50s, and increased its appetite for the growing wave of films from abroad._

Elizabeth Taylor

Ingenue Elizabeth Taylor metamorphosed into a mature actress and the personification of glamorous sexuality in 1951's A Place in the Sun _(right). The 17-year-old violet-eyed beauty played a pampered, seductive society girl whose love affair with a poor man ends tragically. America, critics included, adored her in the part._ Look _magazine said, "Miss Taylor reveals an understanding of passion and suffering that is electrifying." She won acclaim for her role in_ Giant _five years later and again for_ Cat on a Hot Tin Roof _in 1958. Before the decade was out, Taylor appeared in more than a dozen movies; chalked up three marriages, three children, and two divorces; and was widowed when her third husband, Mike Todd, died in a plane crash._

The New Matinee Idols

Audiences were electrified by Marlon Brando's performance in *A Streetcar Named Desire*, first on Broadway and then on film, in 1951. He played the brutish, inarticulate Stanley Kowalski with a raw sexual heat that made stage and screen alike smolder, and the critic for *The New York Herald Tribune* declared that Brando was "as close to perfect as one could wish." The truthfulness of the performance led some people to identify Brando with the aggressive vulgarian he played. "I was the antithesis of Stanley Kowalski," he protested. "I was sensitive by nature and he was coarse."

Of the scores of admiring actors who tried to emulate Brando, only one—James Dean—became an idol in his own right *(pages 48-49)*. Playing moody, sensitive young outsiders, he completed just three memorable movies—*East of Eden*, *Rebel Without a Cause*, and *Giant*—before his untimely death in 1955.

The Many Faces of Brando
The Men (1950)
A Streetcar Named Desire (1951)
Viva Zapata! (1952)
Julius Caesar (1953)
The Wild One (1953)
On the Waterfront (1954)
Desirée (1954)
Guys and Dolls (1955)
The Teahouse of the August Moon (1956)
Sayonara (1957)
The Young Lions (1958)

Flouting the current standards of proper dress, male fans took to wearing T-shirts as Marlon Brando did in A Streetcar Named Desire *(opposite). James Dean (below) shared star billing in* Giant *with Elizabeth Taylor and Rock Hudson.*

Movie Memories

American icons Henry Fonda, John Wayne, and Katharine Hepburn are a few of the stars advertised on the sampling of movie posters shown here. Ronald Reagan starred in the light comedy at lower right in his pre-presidential days.

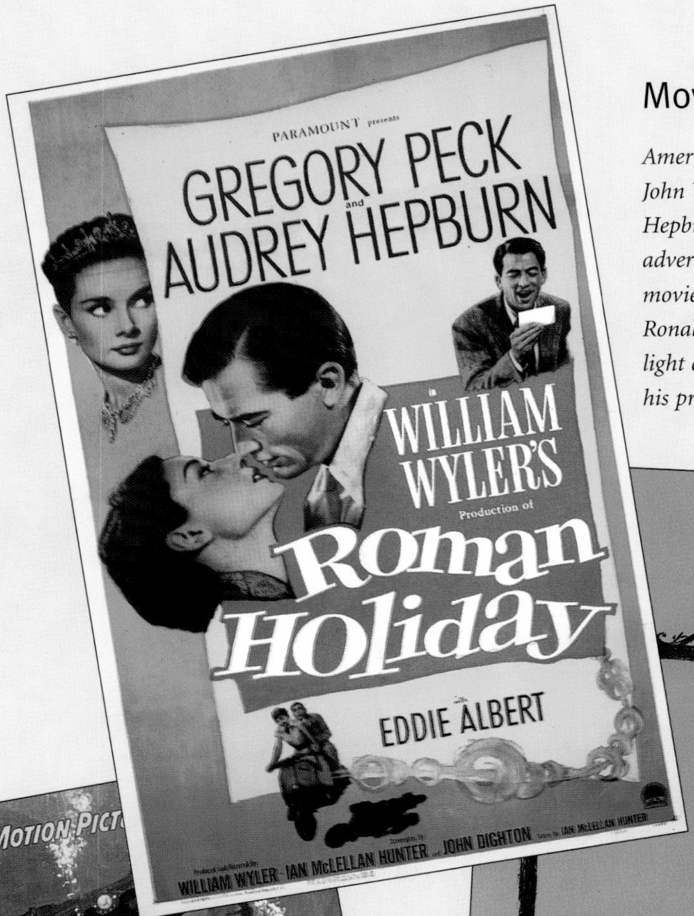

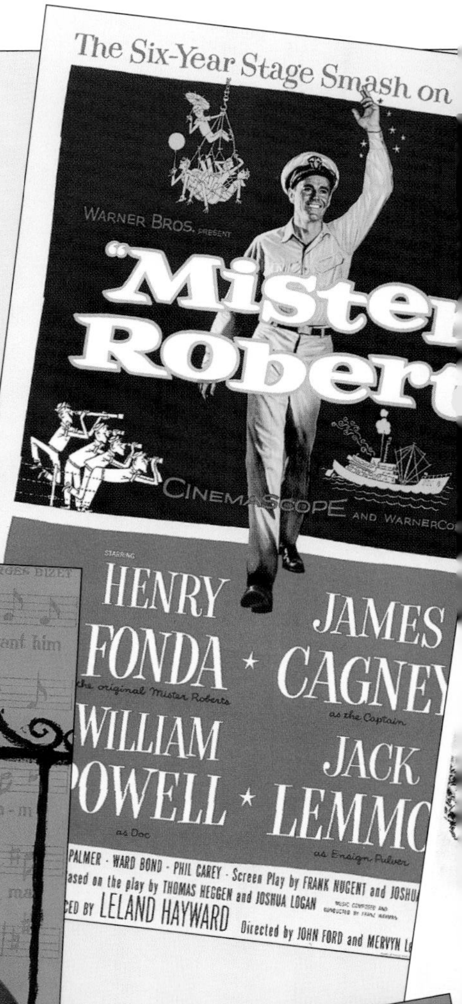

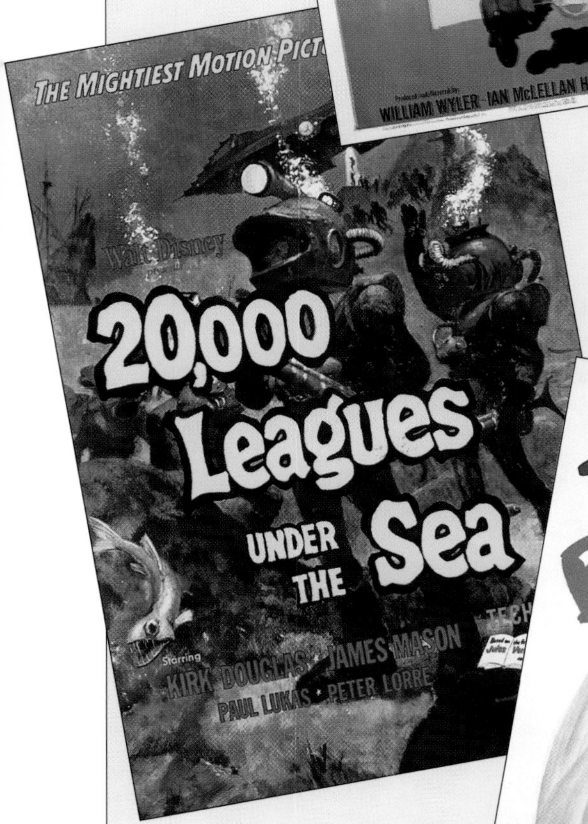

Art Goes Modern

After the war, the capital of the art world shifted from war-ravaged Paris to New York. As the '50s began, the most influential group of painters, led by Jackson Pollock *(right),* were the abstract expressionists. They turned their backs firmly on the longstanding tradition of representation and saw their paintings as vehicles of total personal expression. Pollock discouraged people from attempting to seek something recognizable—the hint of a message—in his canvases. "It's just like looking at a bed of flowers," he said. "You don't tear your hair out over what it means."

While the abstract expressionists were being lionized, Young Turks working in shabby studios were preparing to challenge their supremacy. The chief rebels were Robert Rauschenberg and Jasper Johns, who rejected abstract expressionism in favor of their own innovative versions of representational art *(page 136).* Meanwhile, architects like Frank Lloyd Wright were creating new exhibition spaces devoted exclusively to modern art *(page 137).*

Pollock in Action

Jackson Pollock uses a stick to drip enamel paint onto a canvas spread on the ground (above). His technique of pouring, splashing, flicking, and dribbling paint as he attacked the canvas from all sides came to be known as action painting. Detractors labeled him "Jack the Dripper" and said his pictures looked like tangled hair or macaroni. By the '50s, however, museums and collectors were eagerly buying his work. The 18-foot-wide Blue Poles (above, right), painted in 1952, is considered a masterpiece.

"It's just like looking at a bed of flowers. You don't tear your hair out over what it means."

Jackson Pollock

Art in the Great Outdoors

The garden of the Museum of Modern Art was the place to go in the '50s for anyone who wanted to confront modern sculpture outside and up close (left). Designed by architect Philip Johnson, the tranquil oasis in the middle of Manhattan opened in 1953. A voluptuous nude by Aristide Maillol, The River, reclined at the side of one of two shallow reflecting pools, her hair flowing almost to the water's surface. Other works set among the garden's birches, willows, and winter jasmine included Henry Moore's skeletal Double Standing Figure, seen here behind Maillol's sculpture. In the months following the opening, more than a thousand visitors a day paid the museum's 60-cent admission. Most of them headed straight for the garden to enjoy culture al fresco.

A Gifted Grandma

Anna Mary Robertson "Grandma" Moses (below) had no truck with modern art. In her opinion, abstraction was used to best advantage in "a rug or a piece of linoleum." She started painting at age 78 after arthritis kept her from her chores on her farm in upstate New York. At first she copied Currier and Ives prints. Gaining confidence, she began painting scenes recalled from childhood in her own naive and colorful style. Grandma Moses emerged from small-town obscurity after an art collector spotted several of her pictures on display in a local drugstore window and took them to a Manhattan art dealer. Smitten, the dealer gave her a big show, and the public promptly fell in love, too. Grandma Moses's paintings were exhibited all over the United States and reproduced on china, fabrics, tiles, and greeting cards (above).

On Target

For most of the '50s Jasper Johns, a transplanted South Carolinian, was just one more unknown painter on the fringe of the New York art world. The abstract expressionists dominated the scene, but Johns was inspired by a different muse. He painted simple, familiar symbols and signs—the American flag (below), numbers, letters, targets—generally one per canvas. These ready-made images appealed to Johns because, he explained, "looking at a painting should not require a special kind of focus like going to church. A picture ought to be looked at the same way you look at a radiator."

Johns and Robert Rauschenberg, a fellow southerner and aspiring artist, met in 1954 and became good friends. Rauschenberg helped Johns get his first one-man show in 1958; it was a sensation and a sellout. The Museum of Modern Art bought four of the paintings, and Johns became a leading light of the avant-garde.

An Unusual Palette

Robert Rauschenberg bemused some viewers and incensed others by using paint and objects he found on the streets—chairs, bricks, newspaper clippings, letters, ladders, bed linens, traffic signs, rags, Coke bottles, old radios—to make works for which he coined the name "combines." At right is Monogram, which links a paint-daubed stuffed goat and an automobile tire like the letters of a monogram. For another combine, a life-sized work entitled Bed, Rauschenberg used a quilt, a pillow, part of a sheet, and quantities of paint. An article in Newsweek magazine charged that Bed recalled "a police photo of the murder bed after the corpse has been removed." The association puzzled Rauschenberg. Bed was, he said, one of his "friendliest" works: "My fear has always been that someone would want to crawl into it."

Drama on Fifth Avenue

The Solomon R. Guggenheim Museum (left), designed by Frank Lloyd Wright and completed in 1959 after the architect's death, stands in stark contrast to the neighboring buildings on New York City's Fifth Avenue. A conch shell inspired Wright's design for the museum's exhibition space. Shaped like a broad, hollow cone, it features a sloping ramp that spirals down for seven stories beneath a wide glass dome. To view the collection of 20th-century sculpture and paintings displayed against the gently curved walls, museumgoers take an elevator to the top and stroll down the ramp.

Even before its completion, the building promised to stir up more controversy than the modern works within it. Critics compared it to a washing machine, a pencil sharpener, an eggbeater, and a hair dryer. Wright relished the furor he provoked. "They'll be figuring out this one for years," he chuckled.

Hardcover Bestsellers

Nonfiction

1950 *Betty Crocker's Picture Cook Book* — 300,000

1951 *Look Younger, Live Longer,* Gayelord Hauser — 287,000

1952 *The Holy Bible: Revised Standard Version* — 2,000,000

1953 *The Holy Bible: Revised Standard Version* — 1,100,000

1954 *The Holy Bible: Revised Standard Version* — 710,000

1955 *Gift from the Sea,* Anne Morrow Lindbergh — 430,000

1956 *Arthritis and Common Sense,* Revised Edition, Dan Dale Alexander — 255,000

1957 *Kids Say the Darndest Things!* Art Linkletter — 175,000

1958 *Kids Say the Darndest Things!* Art Linkletter — 225,000

1959 *'Twixt Twelve and Twenty,* Pat Boone — 260,000

Fiction

1950 *The Cardinal,* Henry Morton Robinson — 588,000

1951 *From Here to Eternity,* James Jones — 240,000

1952 *The Silver Chalice,* Thomas B. Costain — 221,000

1953 *The Robe,* Lloyd C. Douglas — 188,000

1954 *Not as a Stranger,* Morton Thompson — 178,000

1955 *Marjorie Morningstar,* Herman Wouk — 191,000

1956 *Don't Go Near the Water,* William Brinkley — 165,000

1957 *By Love Possessed,* James Gould Cozzens — 217,000

1958 *Doctor Zhivago,* Boris Pasternak — 500,000

1959 *Exodus,* Leon Uris — 400,000

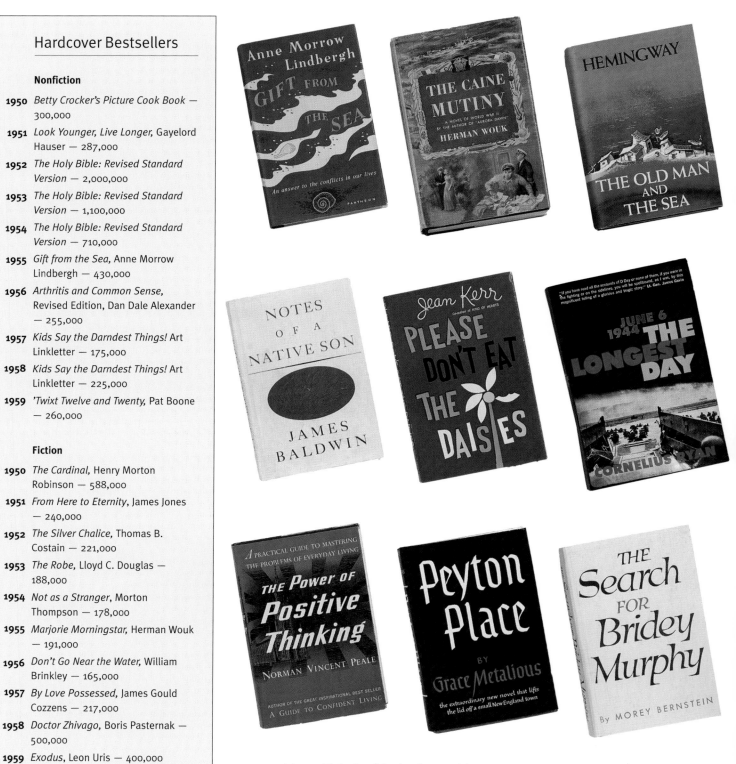

Memorable books of the decade ranged from James Baldwin's look at the black experience in America to preacher Norman Vincent Peale's upbeat self-help guide.

A Boom in Books

Book publishers who gloomily predicted that television would make reading a bygone entertainment happily ate their words when they totaled the decade's sales: Americans had bought 53 percent more books than they had bought during the previous 10 years. The chairman of the board of Simon & Schuster actually thanked TV for the boom. Americans stayed at home to watch their favorite show, he said, and when the show was over, it was "too late to go out and too early to go to bed." So they read.

With such a wealth of customers, publishers could afford to gamble on unknown authors like New Hampshire housewife Grace Metalious. Her first novel, *Peyton Place,* was a sensational—some said scandalous—success. Set in a small New England town, Metalious's lurid soap opera stripped away the prim facade to reveal a secret life of adultery, rape, lust, teenage sex, women who enjoyed sex, incest, drunkenness, greed, vengefulness, and murder. One influential critic labeled the book a "small town peep show," and parents forbade their children to read it. But the peep show was irresistible, and within a year and a half of publication it sold six million copies, most of them in paperback. Copies were passed around until they were dog-eared, and kids switched covers to evade detection.

Another racy commotion was set off by biology professor Alfred Kinsey's *Sexual Behavior in the Human Female,* the 1953 sequel to his volume on males. According to his survey, American women weren't behaving as their parents, husbands, and pastors liked to think. The book was an affront to conventional notions; worse, it might give the innocent ideas. Evangelist Billy Graham declared, "It is impossible to estimate the damage this book will do to the already deteriorating morals of America," and the *Chicago Tribune* denounced Kinsey as a "real menace to society."

The Kinsey report zoomed onto the bestseller list with 200,000 copies sold in four months, at $8.00 each—more than twice the average $3.50 price for a hardcover book. The guardians of morality could, however, take solace in the fact that a new version of the Bible released the year before sold far better.

Some Like It Violent

"It isn't in the best of taste but it will sell." So said the editor of I, the Jury, the 1947 novel in which author Mickey Spillane (above) introduced Mike Hammer, a trigger-happy detective who drew women like flies to honey. Critics called it trash, but the book sold an unprecedented three million paperback copies. Spillane went on to crank out a string of titillating titles such as My Gun Is Quick *and* Kiss Me, Deadly *(inset) in which Hammer, a self-appointed agent of justice, left a slew of corpses belonging to pornographers, Communists, dope peddlers, and other low-life malfeasants. By 1956, seven of the 10 best-selling fiction titles in the history of American publishing were Spillane potboilers.*

The Great White Way

Musicals played to packed theaters as the '50s dawned on Broadway, and cast recordings gave Americans everywhere a taste of the Great White Way. The first smash hit of the decade was *Guys and Dolls,* a funny, slangy look at a colorful bunch of New York gamblers and their girlfriends. The show won accolades for show-stopping songs like "Luck Be a Lady" and "Sit Down, You're Rockin' the Boat."

On the heels of *Guys and Dolls* came *The King and I,* about the prickly relationship between the charming but childish King of Siam and Anna, the British governess. *Pajama Game* was as plebeian as *The King and I* was stylish. Set in a pajama factory, it was packed with great numbers like "Steam Heat" and "Hernando's Hideaway."

The decade's most successful musical was *My Fair Lady,* which opened to ecstatic reviews in 1956. It starred Rex Harrison as Professor Henry Higgins, who teaches a cockney flower seller—

The small-fry band of River City, Iowa, performs "Seventy-Six Trombones" under the baton of music man Harold Hill, who talks the townspeople into buying band equipment.

played by 20-year-old Julie Andrews—to speak like a lady. With 2,717 consecutive performances, it broke all attendance records for musicals in New York.

Another big hit was poles apart in mood and story line. Based on Shakespeare's *Romeo and Juliet*, *West Side Story* transported the story from Italy to a New York slum where the lovers were caught in a feud between rival gangs. Young theatergoers loved the musical, but some traditionalists blasted it for its low-class rumbles and what they considered vulgar lyrics.

Critics of *West Side Story* found *The Music Man* much more palatable. *Time* called Robert Preston "The Pied Piper of Broadway" for his portrayal of Harold Hill, a fast-talking, slightly shady salesman who travels the Midwest peddling brass band instruments to small towns. The jaunty prancing and marching in the old-fashioned musical comedy sent audiences home smiling and humming for 1,375 performances.

Where *The Music Man* was cornfed and clean cut, 1959's *Gypsy* deployed rowdy bumps and grinds and songs like "Everything's Coming Up Roses" to tell the story of America's favorite striptease artist, Gypsy Rose Lee. After closing in New York, star Ethel Merman and the rest of the cast took the show on a triumphant coast-to-coast tour. Closing out the decade was *The Sound of Music*, a warm-hearted smash hit starring Mary Martin.

The King and I: 3/29/51–3/20/54

The dates below each LP cover indicate the musical's initial Broadway run.

The Pajama Game: 5/13/54–11/24/56

Gypsy: 5/21/59–3/25/61

Guys and Dolls: 11/24/50–11/28/53

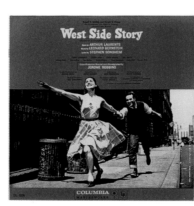

West Side Story: 9/26/57–6/27/59

The Sound of Music: 11/16/59–6/15/63

Rex Harrison listens for Julie Andrews's "h's" as she recites: "In Hartford, Hereford, and Hampshire, hurricanes hardly happen" in My Fair Lady.

The Hit Parade, 1950–1959

1950
1. **Goodnight Irene** Gordon Jenkins and The Weavers
2. **It Isn't Fair** Sammy Kaye
3. **Third Man Theme** Anton Karas
4. **Mule Train** Frankie Laine
5. **Mona Lisa** Nat King Cole
6. **Music! Music! Music!** Teresa Brewer
7. **I Wanna Be Loved** The Andrews Sisters
8. **If I Knew You Were Comin' I'd've Baked a Cake** Eileen Barton
9. **I Can Dream, Can't I?** The Andrews Sisters
10. **That Lucky Old Sun** Frankie Laine

1951
1. **Tennessee Waltz** Patti Page
2. **How High the Moon** Les Paul and Mary Ford
3. **Too Young** Nat King Cole
4. **Be My Love** Mario Lanza
5. **Because of You** Tony Bennett
6. **On Top of Old Smoky** The Weavers
7. **If** Perry Como
8. **Sin (It's No Sin)** Eddy Howard
9. **Come On-a My House** Rosemary Clooney
10. **Mockin' Bird Hill** Patti Page

From Pop to Rock

A new generation of clean-cut singers filled the juke boxes in the '50s, along with perennial favorites like Frank Sinatra and a few Big Bands that lingered on from earlier years. Romantic ballads from solo vocalists like Eddie Fisher, Rosemary Clooney, and Kay Starr, as well as close harmony from quartets like the Four Aces, kept couples dancing cheek to cheek. There were also plenty of fluffy novelties like Patti Page's "The Doggie in the Window," and kids jitterbugged to Teresa Brewer's "Music! Music! Music!" and Rosemary Clooney's swinging "Come On-a My House." An amazingly versatile vocalist, Clooney recorded 31 top-40 hits from 1951 through

Mona Lisa, Mona Lisa, men have named you

Come on-a my house

1954. *Time* magazine put her on its cover, noting approvingly that she sounded "the way pretty girls next door ought to sound."

Other strains in the pop musical mix were the Weavers, serving up fresh versions of traditional songs in a folk-music revival; Les Paul and Mary Ford, pioneering multitrack recording in "How High the Moon" and other hits; Johnnie Ray, the piano-pounding "Million-Dollar Teardrop" whose emotion-soaked renditions of "Cry" and "The Little White Cloud That Cried" got live audiences so fired up that they would storm the stage; and country music star Hank Williams, whose songs of honky tonks and heartbreak—"Hey, Good Lookin'," "Cold, Cold Heart," "Lovesick Blues"—crossed over and picked up fans among pop music devotees.

Another country singer and bandleader, Bill Haley, rocked out

How much is that doggie in the window?

I get misty just holding your hand

1952
1. **Cry** Johnnie Ray
2. **Blue Tango** Leroy Anderson
3. **Any Time** Eddie Fisher
4. **Delicado** Percy Faith
5. **Kiss of Fire** Georgia Gibbs
6. **Wheel of Fortune** Kay Starr
7. **Tell Me Why** The Four Aces
8. **I'm Yours** Don Cornell
9. **Here in My Heart** Al Martino
10. **Auf Wiederseh'n Sweetheart** Vera Lynn

1953
1. **The Song from *Moulin Rouge*** Percy Faith
2. **Till I Waltz Again with You** Teresa Brewer
3. **April in Portugal** Les Baxter
4. **Vaya con Dios** Les Paul and Mary Ford
5. **I'm Walking Behind You** Eddie Fisher
6. **I Believe** Frankie Laine
7. **You You You** The Ames Brothers
8. **The Doggie in the Window** Patti Page
9. **Why Don't You Believe Me** Joni James
10. **Pretend** Nat King Cole

1954
1. **Little Things Mean a Lot** Kitty Kallen
2. **Hey There** Rosemary Clooney
3. **Wanted** Perry Como
4. **Young-at-Heart** Frank Sinatra
5. **Sh-Boom** The Crew-Cuts
6. **Three Coins in the Fountain** The Four Aces
7. **Little Shoemaker** The Gaylords
8. **Oh! My Pa-Pa** Eddie Fisher
9. **Secret Love** Doris Day
10. **Happy Wanderer** Frank Weir

1955
1. **(We're Gonna) Rock Around the Clock** Bill Haley and His Comets
2. **Ballad of Davy Crockett** Bill Hayes
3. **Cherry Pink and Apple Blossom White** Perez Prado
4. **Melody of Love** Billy Vaughn
5. **Yellow Rose of Texas** Mitch Miller
6. **Ain't That a Shame** Pat Boone
7. **Sincerely** The McGuire Sisters
8. **Unchained Melody** Les Baxter
9. **The Crazy Otto** Johnny Maddox and the Rhythmasters
10. **Mr. Sandman** The Chordettes

Pop stars (left to right) Rosemary Clooney, Perry Como, Teresa Brewer, Nat King Cole, Patti Page, and Johnny Mathis were repeat performers in the 1950s hit parade.

1956
1 **Don't Be Cruel** Elvis Presley
2 **The Great Pretender** The Platters
3 **My Prayer** The Platters
4 **The Wayward Wind** Gogi Grant
5 **Whatever Will Be, Will Be** Doris Day
6 **Heartbreak Hotel** Elvis Presley
7 **Lisbon Antigua** Nelson Riddle
8 **Canadian Sunset** Hugo Winterhalter
9 **Moonglow and Theme from** *Picnic*
   Morris Stoloff
10 **Honky Tonk** Bill Doggett

1957
1 **Tammy** Debbie Reynolds
2 **Love Letters in the Sand** Pat Boone
3 **It's Not for Me to Say** Johnny Mathis
4 **Young Love** Tab Hunter
5 **Chances Are** Johnny Mathis
6 **Little Darlin'** The Diamonds
7 **Bye Bye Love** The Everly Brothers
8 **All Shook Up** Elvis Presley
9 **So Rare** Jimmy Dorsey Orchestra
10 **Round and Round** Perrry Como

1958
1 **Volaré (Nel Blu, Dipinto di Blu)**
   Domenico Modugno
2 **It's All in the Game** Tommy Edwards
3 **Patricia** Perez Prado
4 **All I Have to Do Is Dream**
   The Everly Brothers
5 **Bird Dog** The Everly Brothers
6 **Little Star** The Elegants
7 **Witch Doctor** David Seville
8 **Twilight Time** The Platters
9 **Tequila** The Champs
10 **At the Hop** Danny and the Juniors

1959
1 **Mack the Knife** Bobby Darin
2 **The Battle of New Orleans**
   Johnny Horton
3 **Venus** Frankie Avalon
4 **Lonely Boy** Paul Anka
5 **There Goes My Baby** The Drifters
6 **Personality** Lloyd Price
7 **The Three Bells** The Browns
8 **Put Your Head on My Shoulder** Paul Anka
9 **Sleep Walk** Santo and Johnny
10 **Come Softly to Me** The Fleetwoods

of obscurity to a spot on the pop chart in 1954 with his version of "Shake, Rattle, and Roll," which rhythm-and-blues singer Big Joe Turner had made popular among black listeners. Haley's hit was the first loud rumble of what *Life* magazine called a "frenzied teen-age music craze." In 1955 Haley and his group the Comets scored big when featured in *Blackboard Jungle,* a movie about high-school toughs. When the lights came up, the teenagers in the audience were itching to rock around the clock; the adults were shaking their heads. That same year, singer-songwriter Chuck Berry *(below)* stepped up the heat with "Maybellene." His next big hit, "Roll Over Beethoven," released in 1956, announced the rock and roll revolution in no un-certain terms: "Roll over, Beethoven, and tell Tchaikovsky the news!"

Rock and roll had arrived, and with it a new superstar named Elvis Presley. A 21-year-old from Memphis, Tennessee, Elvis made the leap from regional to national stardom in 1956, letting fly a rapid-fire string of million-copy singles beginning with "Heartbreak Hotel" and including "Don't Be Cruel" and "Hound Dog." Journalists, church-men, and parents reacted wrathfully, especially after Elvis appeared on television. Newspaper columnist Eddie Condon de-nounced Elvis for behaving "like a sex maniac in public before millions of impressionable kids." An early fan recalls asking his mother what was "so horrible" about Elvis. She snapped, "Because he's sleazy, is why! Calling a lady a hound dog! And using *ain't.* It's disgusting."

Although the airwaves were being inundated by rock and roll, there was still room for new stylists like Johnny Mathis, who had to choose between a contract with Columbia Records and a spot on the 1956 Olympic track team.

The sampling of records opposite recalls the diversity of '50s rock stars and sounds.

Television's Golden Age

★

HOOKED ON THE TUBE

There are some things a son or daughter won't tell you," the members of the American Television Dealers and Manufacturers Association told parents in a 1950 newspaper ad. "Do you expect him to blurt out the truth—that he's really ashamed to be with the gang—because he doesn't see the same shows they see?"

Howdy Doody, kids wanted their folks to know, had been on the air for three years by then *(page 168)*. Hopalong Cassidy had been riding Topper at the video version of the Bar 20 Ranch for one. What's more, Ed Sullivan was in his second season as emcee of the variety show *Toast of the Town*, comedians George Burns and Gracie Allen had just made the switch from radio, and Milton Berle was well on his way to earning the title "Mr. Television" *(page 157)*. So many Americans were tuning in to his show, the *Texaco Star Theater*, that on November 2, 1948, NBC delayed the broadcast of the Dewey-Truman presidential race until after he had wished his fans good night.

In truth, only 9 percent of American households, about a million, owned "that piece of furniture that stares back at you," as Bob Hope called it. And the four networks—dominant NBC and CBS, newcomer ABC, and short-lived Du Mont—had scheduled programming only in the evening; the rest of the day

One of the decade's best programs, I Love Lucy gave families good reason not just to gather around the television set but, after the introduction of TV dinners (above), to eat there, too.

The Red Skelton Show, 1951-1971

Television test pattern

See It Now, 1951-1958

viewers saw a test pattern *(left, center)*. Yet as the decade began, the new medium's promise seemed obvious and immense. "Can you deny television to your children any longer?" the television dealers asked. "Youngsters today need television for their morale as much as they need fresh air and sunshine for their health."

"If the television craze continues . . . we are destined to have a nation of morons."

Boston University president Daniel Marsh, 1950

Motivated by such appeals—as well as by Uncle Miltie—Americans by the thousands began purchasing television sets, and the networks started competing to entertain the masses. The result was a golden age—a time of fantastic growth, joy, and invention whose herald was Lucille Ball *(pages 158-159)*.

Dancing Old Gold Cigarette Pack from TV ad

Appearing in *I Love Lucy* in 1951, the year in which viewers of Edward R. Murrow's news program *See It Now (left, bottom)* watched network television's first coast-to-coast broadcast, Ball became an instant celebrity in New York, in San Francisco, and everywhere in between. Monday nights at nine, week after week, millions of families dropped everything to watch her and her real-life husband Desi Arnaz play the roles of Lucy and Ricky Ricardo. Number one in New York in just four months, the show became so popular nationwide that Marshall Field, a Chicago department store, switched its weekly clearance sale from Monday to Thursday. A sign in its window attested to a common sentiment: "We love Lucy too, so we're closing on Monday nights."

Eager to fill hours of airtime when Lucy wasn't on, the networks in 1951 also presented more live dramas than Broadway *(pages 162-163)* and invested in expensive, one-time-only specials, such as Gian Carlo Menotti's *Amahl and the Night Visitors,* a nativity opera broadcast on Christmas Eve. *Peter Pan,* a 1955 spectacular starring Mary Martin, drew more viewers than any show to date: 65 million people.

Advertisers were quick to appreciate television's potential—and what it meant for radio. "They had a more potent force available for their selling purposes," observed comic Fred Allen. "Radio was abandoned like the bones at a barbecue." *The Adventures of Superman, Our Miss Brooks, The Adventures of Ozzie and Harriet (pages 160-161),* and *Dragnet (page 165)*—each a successful radio production—all migrated to television in 1952. *The $64,000 Question (page 166)* and *Gunsmoke (page 171)* followed in 1955, joining debutants *The Phil Silvers Show (page 153)* and Jackie Gleason's *The Honeymooners (page 156)* in the networks' dogged search for more and more viewers.

By 1956 Americans owned more than 42 million television sets, and the viewing day had come to include the first 30-minute weekday serials: *As the World Turns* and *The Edge of Night.* Called soap operas because their sponsors were makers of soaps and detergents, the shows were modeled on popular daytime radio programs and targeted at women. They attracted large audiences, humorist James Thurber wrote, by following a simple recipe: "Between thick slices of advertising spread twelve minutes of dialogue, add predicament, villainy, and female suffering in equal measure, throw in a dash of nobility, sprinkle with tears, season with organ music, cover with a rich announcer sauce, and serve five times a week."

As the decade drew to a close, 86 percent of the country's households, or 46 million, had television sets, and average Americans were watching the tube almost six hours a day. The impact of television on everyday life

Most-Watched Shows

1950: Texaco Star Theater (NBC)
1951: Arthur Godfrey's
    Talent Scouts (CBS)
1952: I Love Lucy (CBS)
1953: I Love Lucy (CBS)
1954: I Love Lucy (CBS)
1955: The $64,000 Question (CBS)
1956: I Love Lucy (CBS)
1957: Gunsmoke (CBS)
1958: Gunsmoke (CBS)
1959: Gunsmoke (CBS)

*Toast of the Town /
The Ed Sullivan Show,
1948-1971*

was inescapable: Surveys reported that Americans were staying up later, forsaking traditional meals in the kitchen or dining room for TV dinners in the living room, even timing their use of the toilet with commercial and station breaks.

Critics dubbed television "chewing gum for the mind" and "the real opiate of the people." They wisecracked that watching television "permits people who haven't anything to do to watch people who can't do anything." And child psychologists touched a nerve when they wondered if the growing number of violent programs might be causing children to "grow up with a completely distorted sense of what is right and wrong in human behavior."

But such naysayers did little to dissuade most American television viewers. Charmed when they heard Jimmy Durante wish Mrs. Calabash a good night (wherever she was) or each time George Burns ended his show with "Say good night, Gracie," they continued to tune in. "Television," *See It Now* producer Fred Friendly said, "can show you the Atlantic and the Pacific, and television can show you the face of the moon. But it can also show you the face and heart of man. And perhaps what it does best is the latter."

The Honeymooners, 1955-1956

The George Burns and Gracie Allen Show, 1950-1958

Peter Pan, 1955

Our Miss Brooks, 1952-1956

*The Adventures of
Superman*, 1952-1957

Amos 'n' Andy, 1951-1953

The Phil Silvers Show, 1955-1959

Weekly Schedule

The following list, from a newspaper published in April 1953, shows highlights of what a New Yorker could have found on CBS (channel 2), NBC (4), ABC (7), and other channels.

Saturday

6:30-7 WHAT IN THE WORLD: Dr. Sherman Lee, Curator of Oriental Art at Cleveland Museum, Guest-(2)

7-7:30 PAUL WHITEMAN TEEN CLUB: With Nancy Lewis-(7)

7:30-8 BEAT THE CLOCK: With Bud Collyer-(2)

7:30-8 JOHNNY JUPITER: Satirical Fantasy, on American Life, as Seen by Inhabitants of Planet Jupiter-(5)

8-9 JACKIE GLEASON SHOW: Jan Peerce, Guest-(2)

8-9 ALL-STAR REVUE: With George Jessel, Eddie Cantor, Fred Allen, Gloria De Haven, Guests-(4)

8:30-9 INTERNATIONAL MOTOR SPORTS SHOW: From Grand Central Palace-(11)

9-9:30 THIS IS SHOW BUSINESS: Clifton Fadiman, Host; Jacqueline Susann, Nat Cole, Nora Kaye, Guests-(2)

Hit Parade Singers

9-10:30 SHOW OF SHOWS: With Sid Caesar, Imogene Coca, Marguerite Piazza, Hostess-(4)

9- LIGHTWEIGHT BOUT: Johnny Gonsalves vs. Virgil Akins, from Chicago's Rainbow Arena-(7)

10:30-11 IT'S NEWS TO ME: Panel Quiz, John Daly-(2)

10:30-11 YOUR HIT PARADE: With Snooky Lanson, Dorothy Collins, June Valli-(4)

10:30-11 AMERICA SPEAKS: "Korean Truce—What It Means to Our Economy"—Ben Limb, Ambassador at Large to the U.N., Guest; Don Passante, Moderator-(9) (Première)

Sunday

6:30-7 SEE IT NOW: With Edward R. Murrow, Narrator-(2)

7:30-8 MR. PEEPERS: WALLY COX-(4)

7:30-8:30 OPERA CAMEOS: "Cavalleria Rusticana," With Rina Telli, Soprano; Martha Lipton, Mezzo-Soprano; Jon Grain, Tenor; Richard Torigi, Baritone-(11)

8-9 TOAST OF THE TOWN: Ed Sullivan; Notre Dame Glee Club; Gracie Fields, Cab Calloway, Others, Guests-(2)

9-9:30 FRED WARING SHOW-(2)

9-10 TELEVISION PLAYHOUSE: "Young Lady of Property," Kim Stanley-(4)

10-10:30 ARTHUR MURRAY SHOW: With Charles Coburn, Lisa Kirk, Christine Jorgensen, Guests-(5)

10:30-11 WHAT'S MY LINE-(2)

Monday

8-8:30 GEORGE BURNS AND GRACIE ALLEN-(2)

8-8:30 PAUL WINCHELL-JERRY MAHONEY-(4)

8:30-9 ARTHUR GODFREY TALENT SCOUTS-(2)

8:30-9:30 METROPOLITAN OPERA JAMBOREE: Symphony Orchestra; Soloists: Deems Taylor, Howard Dietz; Others-(7)

9-9:30 "I LOVE LUCY": Lucille Ball and Desi Arnaz-(2)

9-9:30 EYEWITNESS-MYSTERY: "Apartment 4D," With Nita Talbot; Lee Bowman, Host-(4)

9-9:30 NEWS-O-RAMA: Columbia University Forum-(11)

9:30-10 RED BUTTONS SHOW: Gisele MacKenzie, Guest-(2)

9:30-10:30 ROBERT MONTGOMERY PRESENTS: "Second-Hand Sofa," With Ann Rutherford, Leslie Nielsen-(4)

10-11 STUDIO ONE: "Shadow of the Devil," With Mercedes McCambridge and James Dunn-(2)

Arthur Godfrey and Tony Marvin

Tuesday

7:30-7:45	THE DINAH SHORE SHOW-(4)
8-9	ERNIE KOVACS SHOW: With Dorothy Richards, Eddie Hatrak, Trigger Lund and Andy McKay-(2)
8-9	STAR THEATRE: With Milton Berle, Cesar Romero, Laraine Day, Kathryn Murray, Guests-(4)
8-8:30	BISHOP FULTON J. SHEEN-(5)
8:30-9	THE BIG ISSUE: "Should Communists Be Permitted to Teach in Colleges?"—Corliss Lamont, James Burnham-(5)
9-9:30	CITY HOSPITAL: With Melville Ruick-(2)
9-9:30	FIRESIDE THEATRE: "Cocoon," Barbara Brown-(4)
9-	FEATHERWEIGHT BOUT: Bill Bossio vs. Miguel Berrios, from Ridgewood Grove, Brooklyn-(7)

Mama's Judson Laire and Peggy Wood

Ernie Kovacs

Wednesday

7-7:30	MARCH OF TIME: "Omaha, Rail Metropolis on the Plains"-(4)
7:15-7:30	THIS IS CHARLES LAUGHTON: Readings-(11)
7:30-8	DATE WITH JUDY: With Mary Linn Beller-(7)
7:30-8:55	BROADWAY TV THEATRE: "Wuthering Heights," With William Prince, Meg Mundy-(9)
7:45-8	THE PERRY COMO SHOW-(2)
8-9	ARTHUR GODFREY AND HIS FRIENDS: With Frank Parker, Marion Marlowe, Janette Davis-(2)
8-8:30	I MARRIED JOAN: With Joan Davis-(4)
8-9	JUNIOR TOWN MEETING: "Freedom for Enslaved Peoples"—High School Students, Guests-(13)
8:30-9	MUSIC HALL: Patti Page; Ezio Pinza, Guest-(4)
9-10	TELEVISION THEATRE: "Next of Kin," With Frederic Tozere, James Daly, Jack Arthur, Pat Ferris-(4)

Thursday

7-7:15	SAMMY KAYE SHOW: With Jean Martin-(4)
7:30-7:45	DINAH SHORE SHOW-(4)
7:45-8	JANE FROMAN'S U.S.A. CANTEEN-(2)
8-8:30	LIFE WITH LUIGI: Vito Scotti-(2) (Première)
8-8:30	GROUCHO MARX: "You Bet Your Life"-(4)
8:30-9	FOUR-STAR PLAYHOUSE: "Dante's Inferno," With Dick Powell, Regis Toomey-(2)
8:30-9	TREASURY MEN IN ACTION: With Walter Greaza-(4)
8:30-9	CHANCE OF A LIFETIME: Georgie Price, Guest-(7)
9-9:30	VIDEO THEATRE: "With Glory and Honor," With Wendell Corey and Others-(2)
9-9:30	DRAGNET: With Jack Webb-(4)

Friday

8-8:30	MAMA: With Peggy Wood-(2)
8-8:30	DENNIS DAY SHOW: From Hollywood-(4)
8-8:30	ADVENTURES OF OZZIE AND HARRIET-(7)
8:30-9	MY FRIEND IRMA: Marie Wilson, Cathy Lewis-(2)
8:30-9	THE LIFE OF RILEY: With William Bendix, Marjorie Reynolds, and Others-(4)
8:45-9	RUDOLPH HALLEY REPORTS-(7)
9-9:30	PLAYHOUSE OF STARS: "The Mirror," With Victor Jory, Ian MacDonald-(2)
9-9:30	THE BIG STORY: A Reporter's Assignment-(4)
9-9:30	LIFE BEGINS AT EIGHTY-(5, 13)
9-	PRO-BASKETBALL PLAYOFFS: Knickerbockers vs. Minneapolis Lakers, from the 69th Regiment Armory-(11)
9:30-10	OUR MISS BROOKS: With Eve Arden-(2)

Comedians on Screen

Prospecting for as many viewers as possible, television in its early years looked back in time and found a gold mine: the theatrical variety show. Merging highbrow and low, it catered to practically every taste—and did so at a breakneck pace that guaranteed few, if any, dull moments. It was perfect for the new medium, and for such high-energy, wise-cracking comedians as Milton Berle, Jackie Gleason, Sid Caesar, and Imogene Coca, who were its masters. In their hands, vaudeville became what *Variety* called "vaudeo."

Berle's *Texaco Star Theater,* which debuted on television in 1948, broke the ground, and shows such as *The Jack Benny Show* and *Cavalcade of Stars,* soon to become *The Jackie Gleason Show,* followed hot on its heels. *Your Show of Shows*—starring Sid Caesar, Imogene Coca, Carl Reiner, and Howard Morris—was the first to be performed before a theater audience. Ninety minutes of skits, songs, and spoofs of plays or movies (including one entitled "From Here to Obscurity"), it showcased the talents of Woody Allen, Mel Brooks, Neil Simon, and other promising comedy writers.

Jackie Gleason: "And Away We Go!"

Jackie Gleason, pictured above in a pose made famous on the Cavalcade of Stars, created an array of unforgettable characters, including the mustachioed, top-hatted playboy Reggie Van Gleason III, the wimpy Poor Soul, and Joe the Bartender. The most beloved by far, however, was Brooklyn bus driver Ralph Kramden. An endearing combination of bluster and sentiment, Kramden often bellowed to his implacable wife, played on The Honeymooners by Audrey Meadows, "One of these days, Alice! Pow! Right in the kisser!" Yet he always sang a different tune by show's end. "Baby," he would purr, "you're the greatest."

Milton Berle: Mr. Television

*"Anything for a laugh" was Milton Berle's motto.
That included making as many as six costume changes
during the course of a show. Whether he appeared as a
mincing, bewigged Cleopatra, as Carmen Miranda, or as a
Latin lover, an organ grinder, a gap-toothed rube, or a little old lady,
Berle kept the jokes from his gigantic stock of 850,000 coming fast and
furious. His energy was overwhelming. "I think he ought to be investi-
gated by the Atomic Energy Commission," Bob Hope once joked.*

Sid Caesar and Imogene Coca's Show of Shows

*Vaudeville cohorts from the '40s, Sid Caesar and Imogene Coca (below) had
worked the borscht circuit from the Catskills to Florida before they appeared
together on Your Show of Shows. They portrayed the ideal mismatched couple,
the Hickenloopers. Caesar, the "Man of a Thousand Accents," also effortlessly
assumed the personae of writer Somerset Winterset, jazz musician Progress
Hornsby, and German scholarly professor Sigmund von Fraidy Katz.*

Everybody Loves Lucy

Few shows have made a bigger splash than *I Love Lucy,* which premiered in 1951, and no one was quicker to admit it than Red Skelton, whose own show debuted the same year. Skelton won Emmys for best comedy program and best comedian, yet noted at the awards ceremony that he wasn't the funniest act on television. "I don't deserve this," he said, with one of the much-sought-after trophies in hand. "It should go to Lucille Ball."

The prima donna of slapstick comedy, Lucille Ball was irresistible as the harebrained Lucy, who was forever plunging into daffy schemes that inflamed her excitable husband. There was something for everybody to laugh at. Children too young to follow the plots doubled up over Lucy's getting a pie thrown in her face or corralling a flock of baby chicks in her house. As for adults, they loved both the pratfalls and the good-natured fun the show poked at the idiosyncrasies of married life.

Lucy Ricardo doll

Biting Off More Than They Can Chew

In a 1952 episode, Lucy (right) and best friend Ethel abandon home-making to wrap chocolates in a candy factory. A conveyor belt delivers candies faster than they can wrap, and they frantically cram the excess into their mouths as the forewoman yells, "Speed it up a little!"

Lucy disguises herself for a blind date with Ricky.

A Look photographer catches Lucy in a hillbilly getup.

Lucy clowns around with seltzer and a custard pie.

Family Comedies

Already known from radio as "America's favorite couple," Ozzie and Harriet Nelson headed up America's favorite family after they debuted on television with their sons in 1952. Featuring scripts written by Ozzie that were drawn from his family's real life, *The Adventures of Ozzie and Harriet* ran 14 seasons, long enough for both boys to grow up and get married, and for younger brother Ricky to become a teen idol rivaling Elvis Presley. (His version of "I'm Walkin'" sold a million records the week after he sang it on the show.)

Several programs borrowed the Nelsons' formula, including *Make Room for Daddy, Leave It to Beaver,* and *Father Knows Best.* Each one offered real parents, sons, and daughters the opportunity to watch their on-screen counterparts bumble into harmless predicaments, grope for solutions, and then breathe sighs of relief when matters were finally set right—thanks, more often than not, to the mother. "You know, Mom, when we're in a mess," said the Beaver, as if speaking for all of television's kids, "you kind of make things seem not so messy."

Supervisor of the boys' wardrobe and set decorator Harriet pours tea for producer, director, writer, and husband Ozzie, while Ricky (right) and David wait politely to dig in.

"Critics have complained that everyone on our show is a nice person. I don't quite understand this type of complaint."

Ozzie Nelson

Make Room for Daddy, 1953-1957

Leave It to Beaver, 1957-1963

Father Knows Best, 1954-1963

Theater on Television

Broadcasters in the early years of television faced a dilemma: They had more time to fill than programming to fill it, yet Hollywood was reluctant to supply movies, old or new, to a fledgling but dangerous competitor. So networks were forced to create their own plays, turning to novels for stories and to the theater in New York for playwrights and actors. The resulting shows—written and directed by such luminaries as Rod Serling, Gore Vidal, and Paddy Chayefsky and performed live by Jack Lemmon, Anne Bancroft, and others—were the brightest moments of television's golden age, but they didn't shine for long. Hollywood quickly wooed away the playwrights and actors. And after the development of videotape in 1957 networks came to rely on prerecorded shows, which they could air more than once, earning fatter profits.

Child of Our Time by Michel del Castillo, *Playhouse 90*

Little Moon of Alban by James Costigan, *Hallmark Hall of Fame*

Rod Steiger *(left)* and Nancy Marchand in Paddy Chayefsky's *Marty* on *Goodyear/Philco Playhouse*

Requiem for a Heavyweight by Rod Serling,
Playhouse 90

Twelve Angry Men by Reginald Rose,
Studio One

1984 by George Orwell,
Studio One

The Days of Wine and Roses by J. P. Miller,
Playhouse 90

The Bachelor Party by Paddy Chayefsky,
Goodyear Television Playhouse

The Great Escape by Paul Brickhill,
Philco Television Playhouse

Perry Mason

Few shows were more predictable than Perry Mason, starring Raymond Burr (below). Each episode began with a crime, usually murder, and a falsely accused man or woman in need of an attorney to fight the charges. True to the character created in 1933 by novelist Erle Stanley Gardner, who handpicked Burr for the starring role and signed off on each script, Mason would track down leads and chase red herrings, then make his surprising case—and reveal the true killer—in court. "Perry always wins," Time wrote during the show's third season, "and he does not need legal knowledge so much as a passion for digging up evidence and that scowling, aggressive courtroom demeanor that eventually forces a confession on the witness stand."

Cop Shows and Whodunits

Crime and mystery stories, longtime mainstays of film and radio, quickly became what one early television critic called the "backbone of broadcasting." The shows' plots were often formulaic and the acting was sometimes wooden, but their clue-by-clue pacing encouraged armchair gumshoes to match wits with their favorite characters, and the gunfire and screams never failed to make even distracted viewers stop whatever they were doing and look. "One of television's great contributions," declared Alfred Hitchcock *(right)* with mordant humor, "is that it brought murder back into the home, where it belongs."

Dragnet

Man: *"Lousy, sloppy drunk."*

Friday: *"Don't knock her—she had a good reason to drink."*

Man: *"And what's that?"*

Friday: *"She was married to you."*

This exchange, between a man accused of trying to have his wife killed and detective Joe Friday, the no-nonsense star of Dragnet, is typical of the hard-boiled dialogue that made the program so popular after its premiere in 1952. Created and produced by Jack Webb (above), who also wrote many of the scripts and played Friday, the show attracted as many as 38 million viewers with stories based on cases taken from actual Los Angeles Police Department files. "The story you are about to see is true," announcer George Fenneman said before each episode. "Only the names have been changed to protect the innocent." This apparent realism, Time wrote in 1954, gave Americans "a new appreciation of the underpaid, long-suffering, ordinary policeman" and made toys such as the Dragnet Detective Special (inset) a must-have for young fans.

Alfred Hitchcock Presents

Filmmaker Alfred Hitchcock brought a well-deserved reputation for suspense and surprise to television when Alfred Hitchcock Presents aired for the first time in 1955. For 10 seasons, each episode opened the same way: After the camera dwelled on a profile drawing of Hitchcock's rotund figure, the jowly host intoned a lugubrious "Good e-e-e-e-vening," then introduced that week's "tale with a twist." He liked to tweak the show's sponsors, introducing their commercials as "tedious" or as "one-minute anesthetics." He poses above in a "Christmas present" allegedly given to him in 1957 by an irate advertiser.

Twenty-One

MR. VAN DOREN
ON THE AIR

The producers of Twenty-One hit the jackpot when they persuaded Charles Van Doren to be a contestant. Handsome, brainy, and well-spoken, he was, as the show's creator put it, the kind of guy "you'd love to have your daughter marry." His victory over current champion Herb Stempel on December 5, 1956, made him a national hero and sent the show's ratings sky-high. He appeared 15 times, attracting 25 million viewers, then took home $129,000 and started living the highlife. His celebrity, however, fizzled in 1958, when a congressional subcommittee revealed widespread cheating on quiz shows. His public confession to having been coached shocked the country, including its president. "It was a terrible thing to do to the American people," Eisenhower said.

Quiz and Game Shows

Though early game shows were profitable for the networks and fun to appear on, none of the people lucky enough to play ever got rich doing so. Using the secret word on *You Bet Your Life (below, opposite)*, for instance, earned Groucho's guests only $100—peanuts in comparison with the prizes dangled by *The $64,000 Question*, the only game show to hit number one in the ratings during the decade. Its success inspired a spate of similar big-money shows, including *Tic Tac Dough, Beat the Jackpot,* and NBC's *Twenty-One (left).*

The stunts and challenges cooked up by game-show producers could be as silly as they were demanding. The Beat the Clock contestant above, for instance, is using a rope to lift a ball up the last of three steps. The woman above right has entered an isolation booth on The $64,000 Question and is preparing to rack her brain for an answer worth $8,000. Eager to make an overnight fortune, as many as 20,000 people a week wrote to the show, pleading for a chance to stand in her shoes.

The appeal of What's My Line?, *hosted by John Daly, lay in the questions asked by the cast: Dorothy Kilgallen, Steve Allen, Arlene Francis, and Bennett Cerf.*

What's My Line?

"Are you self-employed?"

"Do you deal in services?"

"Do you work for a profit-making organization?"

"Do people come to you?"

"Men and women? Are they happier when they leave?"

"Do you need a college education to do what you do?"

"Is a product involved? Could I hold it in my hand?"

"Is it bigger than a breadbox? Smaller than an elephant?"

"The one, the only" Groucho Marx, host of You Bet Your Life, *appears on the screen of a Zenith combination television, radio, and record turntable. Marx is peering over his ubiquitous cigar at the toy duck that descended whenever a contestant uttered the secret word.*

TV for Kids: Dogs, Mice, and Puppets

Parents have been worrying about the ill effects of boister-ous children's programming from the first day kids crowd-ed into the Peanut Gallery to watch *The Howdy Doody Show* *(below)*. "Long on action, short on coherence," *Time* magazine wrote about the show in 1950. But like the millions who watched *Captain Kangaroo* or *Kukla, Fran and Ollie,* or thrilled to the ad-ventures of heroes like Lassie and Mighty Mouse, Howdy's young fans were not put off by a skeptical review, and in time even their moms and dads came to appreciate the value of programming that could keep little ones out of mischief, if only for 30 minutes.

Saturday morning was "Howdy Doody Time!" for Buffalo Bob Smith as well as the freckle-faced cowboy puppet and the mute clown Clarabell.

As Captain Kangaroo, Bob Keeshan sang, told stories, and performed simple skits with such flesh-and-blood characters as the farmer, Mr. Green Jeans, and an assortment of puppet friends.

Even multiple cover stories in TV Guide failed to divulge Lassie's secret: She was a he. Six different collies, all of them male, played the role over the life of the show.

"Here I come to save the day!" sang Mighty Mouse (above). Sweetheart of Pearl Pureheart and archrival of Oil Can Harry, Edward G. Robinson Cat, Svengali Cat, and other villains, he headlined the Mighty Mouse Playhouse, a showcase for an assortment of Terrytoon cartoons.

Popular Annette Funicello and guitar-strumming Jimmie Dodd dance with two other mouse-eared Mouseketeers on The Mickey Mouse Club.

Horse Operas

"King of the Cowboys" Roy Rogers and his wife, Dale Evans—the "Queen of the West"—ended all 108 episodes of The Roy Rogers Show with their theme song, "Happy Trails to You."

Having tamed the frontiers of film and radio, cowboys like Hopalong Cassidy, the Lone Ranger, and the Cisco Kid rode tall in the saddle across early '50s television. Affable, brave, and often as handy with a six-string as a six-shooter, the cowboys—and their trusty mounts—proved especially popular with children. Like Gene Autry and his horse, Champion, Roy Rogers and Trigger, and, later in the decade, Zorro on either Tornado or Phantom,

Young fans were sure to collect such official paraphernalia as a Roy Rogers bank, a Zorro lunchbox and thermos, and a Lone Ranger lantern.

Zorro—shown on his black stallion, Tornado—was the masked identity of Don Diego, aristocratic avenger of evil doings in colonial California. Played by Guy Williams from 1957 to 1959, the mysterious swashbuckler would thunder off in the night leaving only a telltale "Z" to mark his passing.

they won young viewers by keeping a song in their heart, a gun at their side, and the bad guys on the run.

Older Americans hoping to meet a gunslinger whose life was more like their own had only to wait until *Gunsmoke* debuted on CBS on September 10, 1955. Its main character, Marshal Matt Dillon *(below, right),* wasn't the quickest draw in Dodge City, but he was a sure shot, and his individualism and rough decency mirrored commonly held notions about what it was that had made America great. Paving the way for *Have Gun Will Travel, The Rifleman, Colt .45,* and many other adult Westerns, Dillon came close to making the horse opera a new kind of national literature. Said one actor at the time: "If Shakespeare were alive today, he'd be writing Westerns."

Jay Silverheels and Clayton Moore played Tonto and the Lone Ranger for almost 16 years, yet never fired a silver bullet in anger.

James Arness (below) had a famous gunslinger to thank for his role as Marshal Matt Dillon on Gunsmoke: He was recommended for the job by film star John Wayne.

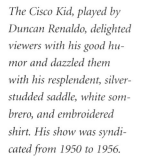

The Cisco Kid, played by Duncan Renaldo, delighted viewers with his good humor and dazzled them with his resplendent, silver-studded saddle, white sombrero, and embroidered shirt. His show was syndicated from 1950 to 1956.

Sport's Decade of Change

★

N O   M O R E   W A I T I N G   T I L L   N E X T   Y E A R

Going nose to nose on the gridiron in helmets without face masks, and swinging at fastballs in caps that shielded them only from the sun, America's athletes in 1950 stood on the threshold of a decade of great change and high hopes.

New protective equipment like batting helmets was only the beginning. Sports figures were soon among the first to fly in commercial jets and perform on television; able to compete wherever the action was and still be seen by the hometown fans, they became national celebrities. And goals long considered unattainable were met when Don Larsen pitched a perfect game in the World Series *(page 175)* and Roger Bannister, a 25-year-old British medical student, broke the four-minute mile *(page 28)*.

The greatest change came as black athletes challenged America's most shameful barrier, racial segregation. Jackie Robinson *(left)* paved the way in the late 1940s. After he won the National League's Most Valuable Player Award in 1949, black players including Willie Mays *(page 175)* and Hank Aaron *(page 179)* took the prize nine times in the next 14 years. By decade's end, other pioneers such as football's Jim Brown, tennis's Althea Gibson *(page 183)*, and basketball's Wilt Chamberlain and Bill Russell *(page 182)* had transformed their sports—and the nation—forever.

Jackie Robinson stops short after dashing down the third baseline during the 1955 World Series. Moments later, he stole home. His deft base running helped the Dodgers win the championship (above), allowing them to shed a reputation as losers, or bums, that they had earned in seven previous World Series losses.

New York Champs

Of the 16 teams playing major league baseball in 1950, three belonged to New York City, and they were three of the best: the American League's Yankees and the National's New York Giants and Brooklyn Dodgers. They fielded 11 of the decade's most valuable players *(right and opposite),* dominated the World Series, and provided a lion's share of baseball's most memorable moments. Three are pictured here, the most dramatic of which was acted out by the 1951 Giants.

With seven weeks to play, they trailed the Dodgers by a seemingly insurmountable margin—13½ games. But unwilling to think about next season, they started winning instead. Taking 37 of the last 44 games, including 16 in a row, they caught their rivals and forced a three-game playoff for the pennant.

The teams split the first two games, and the Dodgers led the third 4-2 when Giants third baseman Bobby Thomson *(right)* stepped to the plate in the bottom of the ninth. There was one out; two men were on base. Manager Leo Durocher spoke for thousands when he pleaded for a home run. "Boy, if you ever hit one," he said, "hit one now."

Most Valuable Players, 1950-1959		
Year	**National League**	**American League**
1950	Jim Konstanty, *Philadelphia*	Phil Rizzuto, *New York*
1951	Roy Campanella, *Brooklyn*	Yogi Berra, *New York*
1952	Hank Sauer, *Chicago*	Bobby Shantz, *Philadelphia*
1953	Roy Campanella, *Brooklyn*	Al Rosen, *Cleveland*
1954	Willie Mays, *New York*	Yogi Berra, *New York*
1955	Roy Campanella, *Brooklyn*	Yogi Berra, *New York*
1956	Don Newcombe, *Brooklyn*	Mickey Mantle, *New York*
1957	Hank Aaron, *Milwaukee*	Mickey Mantle, *New York*
1958	Ernie Banks, *Chicago*	Jackie Jensen, *Boston*
1959	Ernie Banks, *Chicago*	Nellie Fox, *Chicago*

The Shot Heard 'Round the World

Giants third baseman Bobby Thomson watches his three-run homer sail over the left-field fence. The hit capped the greatest comeback in baseball history and gave what Giants fans considered long-overdue comeuppance to the crosstown Dodgers. As Thomson circled the bases, Giants radio announcer Russ Hodges yelled, "The Giants win the pennant! The Giants win the pennant!"

A Giant Catch by Willie Mays

Willie Mays hauls in a 450-foot fly in the eighth inning of the first game of the 1954 World Series, robbing Cleveland Indian Vic Wertz of a sure inside-the-park home run. Mays lost his cap (left) when he then whirled and threw to second. The Indians lost their fight after the play, and the Giants went on to win the game and sweep the series. Fellow outfielder Monte Irvin told Mays that he didn't think he would get to the ball. "You kiddin'?" Mays replied. "I had that one all the way."

World Series Perfect

Yankee catcher Yogi Berra jumps into Don Larsen's arms after the final out of the fifth game of the 1956 World Series. Larsen retired 27 consecutive Dodger batters that day, becoming the only pitcher in series history to throw a perfect game. He seemed an unlikely candidate for such a distinction. Having won just 11 games in the regular season and only nine the year before, he was hardly the Yankees' best pitcher, and his slow ball was so slow, one sportswriter quipped, that "it ought to have been equipped with backup lights." To top things off, Larsen stayed out late drinking the night before the big game. "Damn," said one writer afterward. "The imperfect man just pitched a perfect game."

The Yankee Decade

Well, sirs and ladies, the Yankees have now been mathematically eliminated from the 1949 pennant race," reported a Boston writer before the season began. "They eliminated themselves when they engaged Perfesser Casey Stengel to mis-manage them for the next two years."

Known more for his clowning than his hitting as a player, and for consistently posting losing records as a manager in the '30s and early '40s, Stengel *(opposite, far right)* did seem an odd candidate for the job. Yet un-der his guidance, the Yankees in 1949 won not only the American League pennant, edging out Boston by one game, but also the World Series.

The championship set the stage for the decade to come. Entertained by Stengel's quirky brand of English, which came to be known as Stengel-ese, and powered by the hitting of veterans Yogi Berra and Joe DiMaggio —whose oversized shoes would soon be ably filled by young Mickey Mantle *(right)*—the Yankees went on to win eight of 10 American League pen-nants in the '50s, and six World Series.

The Mick

Called up in 1951 to replace star Joe DiMaggio, Mickey Mantle (above) soon became a new one. "There's never been anyone like this kid," Stengel said. "He has more speed than any slugger and more slug than any speedster—and nobody has ever had more of both of them together."

Mantle's bat and one of 536 balls he hit out of the park

Classic Stengelese

"All right, everybody line up alpha-betically according to your height."

"They say some of my stars drink whiskey, but I have found that the ones who drink milkshakes don't win many ball games."

"I heard it couldn't be done, but it don't always work."

"Now there's three things you can do in a baseball game: you can win or you can lose or it can rain."

"Most ball games are lost, not won."

"I love signing autographs. I'll sign anything but veal cutlets. My ball-point pen slips on cutlets."

"Most of the people my age are dead. You could look it up."

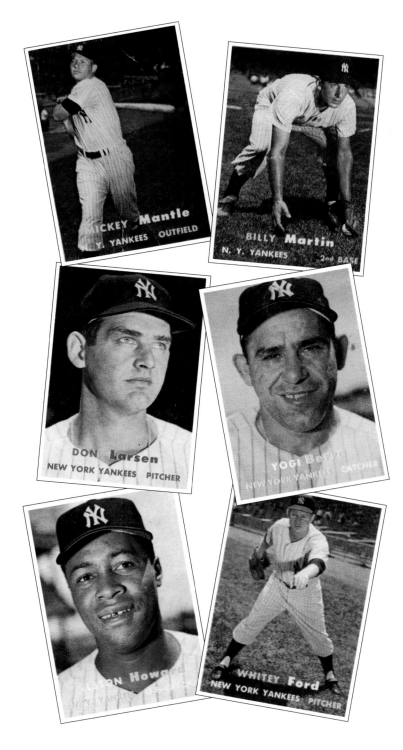

Of the Yankees above, all 1956 World Series champs, only catcher Yogi Berra (right, center) described the game's fine points as well as his manager. "Base-ball," Berra said, "is 90 percent mental. The other half is physical."

Baseball's Best

New Yorkers liked to think they owned the game of baseball in the '50s, and they let the rest of the country know it. When the Yankees faced the Milwaukee Braves in the 1957 World Series, the boys from the Big Apple dubbed their opponents "bush," scornfully equating the club and its fans with minor leaguers.

But Hank Aaron (opposite), a 23-year-old outfielder with powerful wrists who had begun his career in the Negro League with the Indianapolis Clowns, knew better. "Baseball has never seen fans like Milwaukee's in the 1950's and never will again," Aaron recalled fondly. "They were the happiest fans in America. . . . You could pop up with the bases loaded and they would cheer you just for trying."

The smallest of the major league cities, Milwaukee nonetheless set attendance records throughout the decade. Drawing crowds from smaller communities in the region, the city called itself Baseball's Main Street. When Aaron led the Braves to the '57 Series victory in seven games, elated fans unfurled a huge banner proclaiming, "Bushville Wins!"

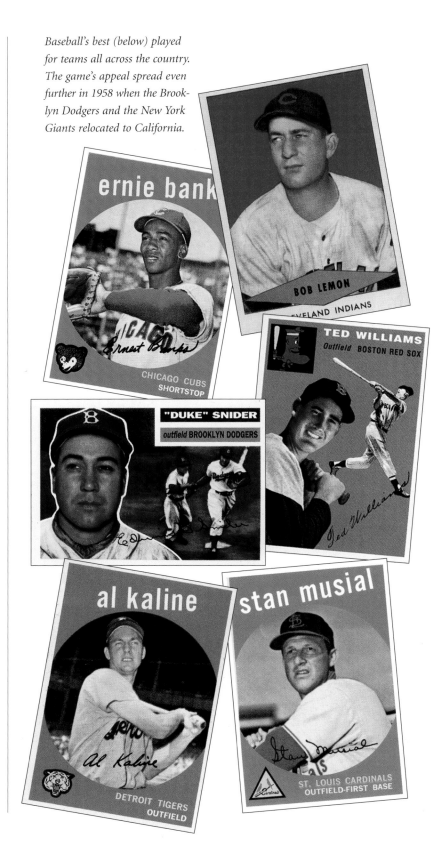

Baseball's best (below) played for teams all across the country. The game's appeal spread even further in 1958 when the Brooklyn Dodgers and the New York Giants relocated to California.

The Ascent of the NFL

The whole country was watching it on TV. . . . That's the game that put the league over the hump," said Baltimore Colts defensive tackle Art Donovan about the 1958 championship between the Colts and the New York Giants that launched America's rapture with pro football.

Broadcast live by NBC to 50 million viewers, the playoff turned the Colts' quarterback Johnny Unitas (*inset, upper right*) and the Giants' halfback Frank Gifford (*inset, upper left*) into household names. When the game went into the first sudden-death overtime ever, to break the 17-17 tie, fans were riveted to their sets. A 12-year-old in Baltimore remembered: "The women were preparing dinner and kept asking, 'When is this going to be over?'" Eight minutes and 15 seconds into overtime, dinner could at last be served; the game ball (*above*) shows the final tally.

At fourth and one on the goal line, fullback Alan Ameche plunges through a gap in the New York Giants' defensive line to give the Baltimore Colts the 1958 NFL title.

Frank Gifford

BACK-GIANTS

John Unitas

BACK-COLTS

Champions With Clout

Television brought new audiences, but it was the athletes themselves who altered the face of several sports during the decade. In basketball, the speed and superb jumping ability of Bill Russell *(right)* shifted the game's tempo from leisurely to rapid-fire and its plane from horizontal to vertical. Even in college he had left his mark, forcing the National Collegiate Athletic Association (NCAA) to develop the "Russell Rule," which widened the foul lane from six to 12 feet in a futile attempt to limit his dominance as an inside shooter and rebounder.

In women's tennis, Althea Gibson *(opposite)* was the catalyst of change. After her debut at Forest Hills in 1950 as the first black woman ever invited to the U.S. Lawn Tennis Association's National Championships, she transformed this once genteel sport with what one observer called her "unladylike gusto." As another commentator noted, "She hits the ball hard and plays like a man. She runs and covers the court better than any of the other women."

Battle of the Titans

The pace of pro basketball accelerated in the '50s thanks to a rule change and two players of extraordinary skill. The 24-second shot clock (below), which limited the amount of time each team had to shoot a basket, led to more action and higher-scoring games. Driving that action and garnering many of those points were six-foot-10-inch Bill Russell (right) and seven-foot-two-inch Wilt Chamberlain (left), by far the best players of their time. Russell led the Boston Celtics to a league championship in 1957 and dominated the pro ranks until 1959, when Chamberlain signed with the Philadelphia Warriors. The face-offs between these two giants became the stuff of hoops legend.

Floor model
24-second shot clock,
vintage 1954

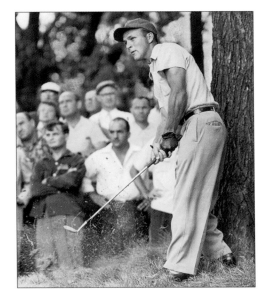

Arnie's First

Twenty-four-year-old Arnold Palmer (left) chips out of the rough in the 1954 U.S. Amateur championship, his first major victory. Four years later he won the Masters tournament and went on to win it three more times. Palmer's no-holds-barred style of play transformed the genteel game into a spectator sport.

Queen of Center Court

Lean, long-limbed Althea Gibson (below) became the first black player to triumph in big-time tennis by winning both Wimbledon and the U.S. National Championship in 1957. Just entering the national invitationals was a feat; shut out by unwritten rules at local tennis clubs for years, she was finally invited to join an all-white club—a move that made her eligible for the nationals.

Exclusive FIGHT PICTURES!

OFFICIAL HEAVYWEIGHT CHAMPIONSHIP FILMS!

JERSEY JOE WALCOTT VS. ROCKY MARCIANO

ROUND-BY-ROUND HIGHLIGHTS!
CLIMAX ACTION IN SLOW-MOTION!

Distributed by
RKO RADIO PICTURES, INC.

The Original Rocky

Rocky Marciano delivers the final blow to Joe Walcott, a solid right to the jaw in round 13 of their 1952 heavyweight title fight in Philadelphia. Although Rocky had a short reach and was not known for finesse, his powerful punching and stamina always won out: He retired in 1956 with the unique distinction of never having lost a professional fight.

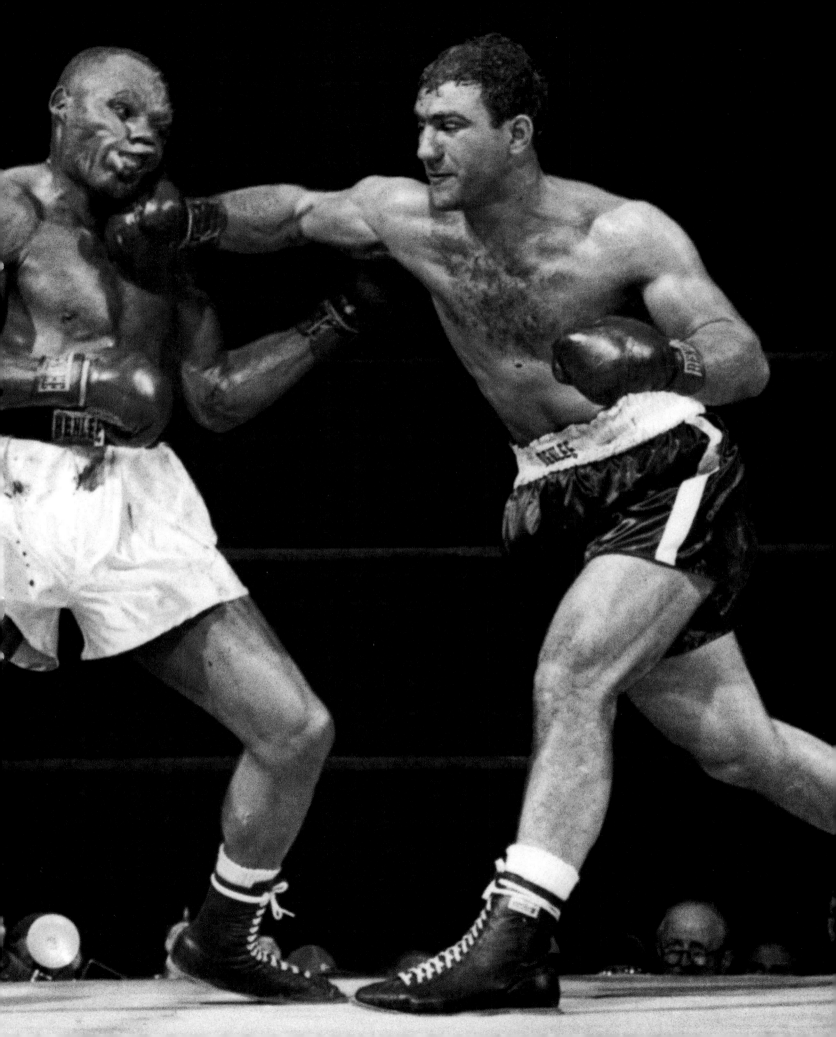

ACKNOWLEDGMENTS

The editors wish to thank the following individuals and institutions for their valuable assistance in the preparation of this volume:
Richard Allen, Upper Montclair, N.J.; Judy and Ed Ashley, Jed Collectibles, Pemberton, N.J.; James Beck, A. J.'s Sports Stop, Vienna, Va.; George Brown, Wyandot Corporation, Marion, Ohio; Daniel Donnelly, Modern Design Studio, Alexandria, Va.; David Hoffman, Los Angeles, Calif.; Charles Jones, Reading, Pa.; Paul D. Ledvina, Mobil Corporation, Fairfax, Va.; George Mansy, Generous George's Positive Pizza and Pasta Place, Alexandria, Va.; Dennis H. J. Medina, Dwight D. Eisenhower Museum, Abilene, Kans.; Jennifer Noonan, Zenith Electronics Corporation, Glenview, Ill.; Jane Steele, Chronicle Books, San Francisco, Calif.; Milo Stewart Jr., National Baseball Hall of Fame and Museum, Cooperstown, N.Y.; George Theofiles, "Miscellaneous Man," New Freedom, Pa.; Pete Vollmer, Annandale, Va.

PICTURE CREDITS

Hirsch, Grand View, N.Y.; © Michael Melford/The Image Bank. **100, 101:** Carl Iwasaki for *Life*—Neal Peters Collection, New York. **102:** Collection of John Baeder—UPI/Corbis-Bettmann. **103:** Courtesy Douglas A. Yorke Jr., co-author of *Hitting the Road: The Art of the American Road Map* (Chronicle Books)(3); ©1997 Michael Karl Witzel/CoolStock—collection of John Baeder; no credit—collection of Dave Lincoln(2); courtesy Mobil Oil Corporation(2)—courtesy Vic's Place, Guthrie, Okla.(2). **104:** Courtesy General Motors Media Archives, Neg. No.X20265-5; Hank Walker for *Life*—UPI/Corbis Bettmann. **105:** Bill Bridges for *Life*. **106:** J. R. Eyerman for *Life*. **108, 109:** UPI/Corbis-Bettmann. **110, 111:** Reprinted with permission of the *Atlanta Daily World*, photo courtesy Library of Congress—Carl Iwasaki for *Life*(2). **112, 113:** Robert Kelley for *Life*. **114:** The Granger Collection, New York. **115:** Dan Weiner, courtesy Sandra Weiner(2)—Don Cravens for *Life*. **116, 117:** AP/Wide World Photos. **118:** Don Cravens for *Life*. **119:** UPI/Corbis-Bettmann—Don Cravens for *Life*. **120, 121:** ©Burt Glinn/Magnum Photos, Inc., New York. **122, 123:** Courtesy Jed Collectibles, Pemberton, N.J.; Philippe Halsman © Halsman Estate. **124:** Bob Willoughby/Globe Photos—courtesy The Wyandot Popcorn Museum, Marion, Ohio, photograph by Lew Lause Studio. **125:** United Artists/Hamilton Projects, Inc. **126, 127:** Courtesy The Kobal Collection, New York. **128:** Courtesy George Zeno; courtesy BFI Stills, Posters and Designs, London—inset courtesy Steven S. Raab Autographs, Ardmore, Pa.—courtesy The Kobal Collection, New York. **129:** Museum of Modern Art, New York; Photos ©1998 Time Life Inc.(2); courtesy BFI Stills, Posters and Designs, London. **130:** Courtesy BFI Stills, Posters and Designs, London. **131:** Photofest, New York. **132, 133:** Hershenson-Allen Archive, West Plains, Mo. **134, 135:** "Jackson Pollock," 1950, photograph by Hans Namuth, ©1991 Hans Namuth Estate, courtesy Center for Creative Photography, The University of Arizona; painting by Jackson Pollock, courtesy National Gallery of Australia, Canberra, © 1997 Pollock-Krasner Foundation/ Artists Rights Society (ARS), New York—Martha Holmes. **136, 137:** Grandma Moses: *A Country Wedding.* Copyright © 1992, Grandma Moses Properties Co., New York—no credit; The Museum of Modern Art, New York. Gift of Philip Johnson in honor of Alfred H. Barr Jr. ©1997 Jasper Johns/Licensed by VAGA, New York, NY; Corbis-Bettmann—Robert Rauschenberg, *Monogram, 1955-59*, Collection Moderna Museet, Stockholm, © Robert Rauschenberg/Licensed by VAGA, New York, NY. **138:** *Old Man and The Sea* courtesy Goodwin House West, Arlington, Va., *The Longest Day* courtesy Florence Coughran, other photos © 1998 Time Life Inc. **139:** Peter Stackpole for *Life*—photo © 1998 Time Life Inc. **140, 141:** Eliot Elisofon for *Life*; courtesy Kermit Bloomgarden. **142:** Courtesy collection of Roland

and Nancy Finken; courtesy Jane Coughran—photos ©1998 Time Life Inc.(3); courtesy Jane Coughran. **143:** Leonard McCombe, inset courtesy Herman Levin. **144, 145:** Background lyrics by Studio A for Time Life Inc.—Michael Ochs Archives, Venice, Calif.(4); Frank Driggs Collection; Michael Ochs Archives, Venice, Calif. **146:** Michael Ochs Archives, Venice, Calif. **147:** Courtesy Val Shively, R&B Records, Upper Darby, Pa. **148, 149:** Courtesy of Campbell Soup Company, Camden, N. J.; SuperStock, Inc., Jacksonville, Fla., inset photo The Everett Collection, New York. **150:** The Everett Collection, New York—Photofest, New York(2); no credit **151:** Culver Pictures Inc., New York. **152, 153:** The Everett Collection, New York(2); no credit—CBS Photo Archive—The Everett Collection, New York; Photofest, New York(2). **154:** Brown Brothers, Sterling, Pa.; CBS Photo Archive. **155:** Ralph Morse for *Life*; Culver Pictures, Inc., New York. **156:** The Everett Collection, New York. **157:** Photofest, New York; Culver Pictures Inc. **158, 159:** Courtesy Hake's Americana & Collectibles, York, Pa.; The Everett Collection, New York; Photofest, New York(2)—Loomis Dean for *Life*. **160, 161:** Neal Peters Collection; ABC—The Everett Collection, New York—Photofest, New York. **162:** Bill Bridges for *Life*—NBC—Culver Pictures Inc., New York. **163:** CBS Photo Archive; no credit—Allan Grant for *Life*; CBS Photo Archive—Culver Pictures, Inc., New York; Brown Brothers, Sterling, Pa. **164:** No credit. **165:** Photofest, New York; Archive Photos, New York—courtesy Hake's Americana & Collectibles, York, Pa. **166:** The Everett Collection, New York—Photofest, New York; The Everett Collection, New York. **167:** Photofest, New York—Michael Beasley, courtesy Zenith Corporation, Glenview, Ill., inset photo from Photofest, New York. **168:** Courtesy Hake's Americana & Collectibles, York, Pa.—Photofest, New York. **169:** Photofest, New York; except *TV Guide* courtesy Hake's Americana & Collectibles, York, Pa. **170:** Movie Still Archives, Harrison, Nebr.—courtesy Hake's Americana & Collectibles, York, Pa.(4); Photofest, New York. **171:** Photofest, New York. **172, 173:** Ralph Morse for *Life*; © October 10, 1955, *The Daily News*, New York. **174:** AP/Wide World Photos. **175:** Milo Stewart Jr./National Baseball Hall of Fame Library, Cooperstown, NY—AP/Wide World Photos; UPI/Corbis-Bettmann. **176:** Hy Peskin—Milo Stewart Jr./National Baseball Hall of Fame Library, Cooperstown, NY(2). **177:** Courtesy Andrew Keegan(6); UPI/Corbis-Bettmann. **178:** Courtesy James Beck, A.J.'s Sport Stop, Vienna, Va. **179:** John Zimmerman for *Sports Illustrated*. **180, 181:** Courtesy Pro Football Hall of Fame; © Wide World Photos/NFL Photos, insets courtesy James Beck, A.J.'s Sport Stop, Vienna, Va.(2). **182, 183:** Steven Freeman/NBA Photos; UPI/Corbis-Bettmann; AP/Wide World Photos—Hulton Getty Collection, London. **184, 185:** Jo Sports, Inc., Brookhaven, N.Y.; UPI/Corbis-Bettmann.

BIBLIOGRAPHY

BOOKS

Aaron, Henry, with Lonnie Wheeler. *I Had a Aammer: The Hank Aaron Story.* New York: HarperCollins Publishers, 1991.

Ambrose, Stephen. *Eisenhower, Volume 2: The President.* New York: Simon & Schuster, 1984.

Andrews, Bart:
    The I Love Lucy Book. New York: Doubleday, 1985.
    The Story of "I Love Lucy." New York: Popular Library, 1976.

Bayley, Edwin. *Joe McCarthy and the Press.* Madison: University of Wisconsin Press, 1981.

The Best of Sports Illustrated. New York: Sports Illustrated, 1996.

Brando, Marlon. *Brando.* New York: Random House, 1994.

Brooks, Tim, and Earle Marsh. *The Complete Directory to Prime Time Network TV Shows: 1946-Present.* New York: Ballantine Books, 1988.

Buege, Bob. *The Milwaukee Braves: A Baseball Eulogy.* Milwaukee: Douglass American Sports Publications, 1988.

Caute, David. *The Great Fear: The Anti-Communist Purge under Truman and Eisenhower.* New York: Simon & Schuster, 1978.

Chronicle of the Cinema. London: Dorling Kindersley, 1995.

Daly, Dan, and Bob O'Donnell. *The Pro Football Chronicle.* New York: Collier Books, 1990.

Denis, Christopher Paul, and Michael Denis. *Favorite Families of TV.* New York: Citadel Press, 1992.

Dickson, Paul (comp.). *Baseball's Greatest Quotations.* New York: Edward Burlingame Books, 1991.

Diggins, John Patrick. *The Proud Decades.* New York: Norton, 1988.

The Fifties: Photographs of America. New York: Pantheon Books, 1985.

Finch, Christopher. *Highways to Heaven.* New York: HarperCollins, 1992.

Flammang, James M., and The Auto Editors of *Consumer Guide. Cars of the Fabulous '50s.* Lincolnwood, Ill.: Publications International, 1995.

Fleischer, Nat, and Sam Andre. *A Pictorial History of Boxing.* New York: Citadel Press, 1993.

Georgano, Nick. *Art of the American Automobile.* New York: Smithmark, 1995.

Gifford, Frank, and Harry Waters. *The Whole Ten Yards.* New York: Random House, 1993.

Goldman, Eric F. *The Crucial Decade—and After: America, 1945-1960.* New York: Vintage Books (Random House), 1960.

Gordon, Lois, and Alan Gordon. *American Chronicle.* New York: Atheneum, 1987.

Gowdy, Curt, with John Powers. *Seasons to Remember.* New York: HarperCollins, 1993.

Gunnell, John A., and Mary L. Sieber (eds.). *The Fabulous '50s: The Cars, the Culture.* Iola, Wis.: Krause Publications, 1992.

Halberstam, David. *The Fifties.* New York: Fawcett Columbine, 1993.

Hart, Jeffrey. *When the Going Was Good!* New York: Crown, 1982.

Hay, Peter. *MGM: When the Lion Roars.* Atlanta: Turner Publishing, 1991.

Heston, Charlton. *In the Arena.* New York: Simon & Schuster, 1995.

Hoffman, David. *Kid Stuff.* San Francisco: Chronicle Books, 1996.

Hornsby, Alton, Jr. *Milestones in 20th-Century African-American History.* Detroit: Visible Ink Press, 1993.

Hughes, Robert. *The Shock of the New.* New York: Knopf, 1996.

Jackson, Lesley. *The New Look.* New York: Thames and Hudson, 1991.

Javna, John. *Cult TV.* New York: St. Martin's Press, 1985.

Kahn, Roger. *The Era: 1947-1957, When the Yankees, the Giants, and the Dodgers Ruled the World.* New York: Ticknor & Fields, 1993.

Kallir, Otto. *Grandma Moses.* New York: Harry N. Abrams, 1973.

Kasher, Steven. *The Civil Rights Movement: A Photographic History, 1954-68.* New York: Abbeville Press, 1996.

Key, Mike, and Tony Thacker. *Fins and the Fifties.* London: Osprey, 1987.

King, Martin Luther, Jr. *Stride Toward Freedom.* New York: Ballantine Books, 1958.

Kinnard, Douglas. *Ike 1890-1990: A Pictorial History.* Washington, D.C.: Brassey's (US), 1990.

Kleinfelder, Rita Lang. *When We Were Young: A Baby-Boomer Yearbook.* New York: Prentice Hall General Reference, 1993.

Kotz, Mary Lynn. *Rauschenberg.* New York: Harry N. Abrams, 1990.

Laufe, Abe. *Broadway's Greatest Musicals.* New York: Funk & Wagnalls, 1969.

Layman, Richard (ed.). *American Decades: 1950-1959.* Detroit: Gale Research, 1994.

Levenstein, Harvey. *Paradox of Plenty.* New York: Oxford University Press, 1993.

McCall, Michael. *The Best of 50s TV.* New York: Mallard Press, 1992.

McDonough, Will, et al. *75 Seasons: The Complete Story of the National Football League, 1920-1995.* Atlanta: Turner Publishing, 1994.

Maltby, Richard, ed. *Passing Parade: A History of Popular Culture in the Twentieth Century.* New York: Oxford University Press, 1989.

Marling, Karal Ann. *As Seen on TV: The Visual Culture of Everyday Life in the 1950s.* Cambridge, Mass.: Harvard University Press, 1994.

Marschall, Rick. *The Golden Age of Television.* New York: Exeter Books, 1987.

Miller, Douglas T., and Marion Nowak. *The Fifties: The Way We Really Were.* Garden City, N.Y.: Doubleday, 1977.

Oakley, J. Ronald. *God's Country.* New York: Dembner Books, 1986.

Our Glorious Century. Pleasantville, N.Y.: Reader's Digest, 1994.

Our Times. Atlanta: Turner Publishing, 1995.

Palmer, Robert. *Rock and Roll.* New York: Harmony Books, 1995.

Patterson, James T. *Grand Expectations: The United States, 1945-1974.* New York: Oxford University Press, 1996.

Perseverance (African Americans: Voices of Triumph series). Alexandria, Va.: Time-Life Books, 1993.

Phillips, Louis, and Burnham Holmes. *The TV Almanac.* New York: Macmillan, 1994.

Reichler, Joseph, and Jack Clary. *Baseball's Great Moments.* New York: Galahad Books, 1990.

Rubin, Nancy. *The New Suburban Woman: Beyond Myth and Motherhood.* New York: Coward, McCann & Geoghegan, 1982.

Scheuer, Steven H. (ed.). *Movies on TV: 1986-1987.* New York: Bantam Books, 1985.

Shadow of the Atom: 1950-1960 (This Fabulous Century series). Alexandria, Va.: Time-Life Books, 1970.

Solomon, Deborah. *Jackson Pollock.* New York: Simon & Schuster, 1987.

Stacy, Tom. *Decades: The Fifties.* Austin, Tex.: Steck-Vaughn, 1990.

Stark, Steven D. *Glued to the Set.* New York: Free Press, 1997.

Steadman, John F. *The Greatest Football Game Ever Played.* Baltimore: Press Box Publishers, 1988.

Stevenson, Janet. *The Montgomery Bus Boycott, December, 1955: American Blacks Demand an End to Segregation.* New York: Franklin Watts, 1971.

Stones, Barbara. *America Goes to the Movies.* North Hollywood, Calif.: National Association of Theatre Owners, 1993.

Tamplin, Ronald (ed.). *The Arts.* Oxford: Oxford University Press, 1991.

Vancil, Mark (ed.). *NBA at 50.* Avenel, N.J.: Park Lane Press, 1996.

Waldie, D. J. *Holy Land.* New York: Norton, 1996.

Whitburn, Joel:
    Joel Whitburn's Pop Hits 1940-1954. Menomonee Falls, Wis.: Record Research, 1994.
    Joel Whitburn's Top Pop Singles 1955-1993. Menomonee Falls, Wis.: Record Research, 1994.

Whittingham, Richard (ed.). *Life in Sports.* New York: Harper & Row, 1985.

Willard, Charlotte. *Frank Lloyd Wright.* New York: Macmillan, 1972.

Williams, Juan. *Eyes on the Prize: America's Civil Rights Years, 1954-1965.* New York: Penguin Books, 1987.

Wilson, Sloan:
    The Man in the Gray Flannel Suit II. New York: Arbor House, 1984.
    What Shall We Wear to This Party? New York: Arbor House, 1976.

Winship, Michael. *Television.* New York: Random House, 1988.

PERIODICALS

"Dwight D. Eisenhower, 1890-1969." *Newsweek,* April 7, 1969.

Life magazine, January 1950-December 1959.

Time magazine, January 1950-December 1959.

TIME® LIFE BOOKS

Time-Life Books is a division of Time Life Inc.

TIME LIFE INC.
PRESIDENT and CEO: George Artandi

TIME-LIFE BOOKS
PRESIDENT: Stephen R. Frary
PUBLISHER/MANAGING EDITOR: Neil Kagan

OUR AMERICAN CENTURY
The American Dream: The 50s

EDITORS: Loretta Britten, Sarah Brash
DIRECTOR, NEW PRODUCT DEVELOPMENT:
Elizabeth D. Ward
MARKETING DIRECTOR: Joseph A. Kuna

Deputy Editors: Jane Coughran, Esther Ferington,
Charles J. Hagner, Sara Mark
Marketing Manager: Janine Wilkin
Picture Associate: Anne Whittle
Copyeditors: Claudia S. Bedwell, Anne B. Farr
Technical Art Specialist: John Drummond
Picture Coordinator: Betty H. Weatherley
Editorial Assistant: Christine Higgins

Design for *Our American Century* by Antonio Alcalá,
Studio A, Alexandria, Virginia.

Special Contributors: Glen B. Ruh, Robert M. S. Somerville,
Robert Speziale (editing); Ronald H. Bailey, Maggie Debelius,
Laura Foreman, Elizabeth Schleichert, Mary-Sherman
Willis (writing); Daniel Kulpinski, Marilyn Murphy Terrell
(research-writing); Susan Borden, Patti Cass (research); Marti
Davila, Richard Friend, Christina Hagopian, Virginia Ibarra-
Garza, Henry Quiroga, Wendy Schleicher (design); Susan
Nedrow (index).

Correspondents: Christine Hinze (London), Christina
Lieberman (New York).

Director of Finance: Christopher Hearing
Directors of Book Production: Marjann Caldwell, Patricia Pascale
Director of Publishing Technology: Betsi McGrath
Director of Photography and Research: John Conrad Weiser
Director of Editorial Administration: Barbara Levitt
Production Manager: Gertraude Schaefer
Quality Assurance Manager: James King
Chief Librarian: Louise D. Forstall

EDITORIAL CONSULTANT
Richard B. Stolley is currently senior editorial adviser at Time
Inc. After 19 years at *Life* magazine as a reporter, bureau chief,
and assistant managing editor, he became the first managing
editor of *People* magazine, a position he held with great success
for eight years. He then returned to *Life* magazine as managing
editor and later served as editorial director for all Time Inc.
magazines. In 1997 Stolley received the Henry Johnson Fisher
Award for Lifetime Achievement, the magazine industry's
highest honor.

Other History Publications:

What Life Was Like
The American Story
Voices of the Civil War
The American Indians
Lost Civilizations
Mysteries of the Unknown
Time Frame
The Civil War
Cultural Atlas

Library of Congress Cataloging-in-Publication Data
The American dream : the 50s / by the editors of Time-Life
Books, Alexandria, Virginia : with a foreword by Hugh Downs.
    p. cm.
Includes bibliographical references and index.
ISBN 0-7835-5500-8
ISBN Trade Edition 0-7370-0201-8
1. United States—History—1945-1953—Miscellanea.
2. United States—History—1953-1961—Miscellanea.
3. Popular culture—United States—History—20th century—
Miscellanea.
I. Time-Life Books.
E813.A766 1998
973.91—DC21   97-44985
                                                   CIP

For information on and a full description of any of the Time-
Life Books series listed above, please call 1-800-621-7026
or write:

Reader Information
Time-Life Customer Service
P.O. Box C-32068
Richmond, Virginia 23261-2068